SO-BPM-883

GRAPE-A-HOL

How Big Business is Subverting Artisan Winemaking and the Future of Fine Wine

by

Michael F. Spratt and Mark L. Feldman

"Abracadabra! . . . FINE WINE! Trust me!"

First published by Dog Ear Publishing
4010 W. 86th Street, Ste H
Indianapolis, IN 46268
www.dogearpublishing.net

ISBN: 978-1-4575-1030-4

This book is printed on acid-free paper.

Printed in the United States of America

ACKNOWLEDGMENTS

As with any enterprise, the final product reflects the hard work and efforts of many people. As the authors we are responsible for the opinions, perspective, and content of this book, but there are many people who have helped make it better by providing useful comments, criticism, and support. We offer special appreciation to the following for their invaluable contributions.

To the team at Destiny Bay Wines – Brett Taylor, Dan Sullivan, Mark Boyle, Ara McGregor, and Fern Kerr – for their hard work day in and day out that reflects the spirit and passion of true artisan winemaking. They are the practitioners who carry on an ancient craft and offer inspiration to us all.

To Sean Spratt, the owner, General Manager, and winemaker at Destiny Bay for his persistence and patience. Not only do all problems stop at his desk, but his multi-faceted talent keeps everything from winemaking to email running with a precision that small businesses seldom enjoy. His uncompromising commitment to quality and the essence of the Destiny Bay brand is a testament to artisan principles.

To Ann Spratt, Destiny Bay's co-founder and chief wine scientist, for her special talents and knowledge. We could not have written this book without her impressive ability to keep complex issues from sounding confusing. Were it not for her insights and technical assistance this book would have certainly lost its footing.

To Adele Feldman, for her moral support and insights that helped us see many of the issues more clearly. Without her sense of humor, passion, and enthusiasm for Destiny Bay we may well have wandered off into a self-absorbed writer's oblivion.

And finally to the thousands of artisan winemakers around the world, we offer our respect and admiration. These fearless individuals embody the spirit of artisan winemaking. Without their dedication and effort that magical bond between people and the earth that produces wine would be lost to us all.

CONTENTS

PREFACE

The essays in this book address concerns shared by many small artisan winemakers which are debated by participants up and down the supply chain. The references are drawn from publicly available sources and apply to businesses located in major wine regions all over the world. The opinions are largely our own, but they are widely shared. Most of the examples are drawn from New Zealand and the United States, however, and this is for two simple reasons.

First, we were raised in the U.S., and lived in the region that is home to Napa Valley and the many other notable Northern California appellations. Second, our own vineyard and winery, Destiny Bay, is located on Waiheke Island, New Zealand. In short, we are writing about what we know.

The U.S. is presently the largest wine market in the world. The total retail value of all wines (domestic, imported, still, sparkling, and fortified) sold in the U.S. in 2012 is projected to be U.S.$44 billion.[1] There are approximately 8,000 domestic brands and 7,626 wineries in the U.S.,[2] with 3,519 in California alone.[3] In 2010, roughly 250,000 wine labels from around the world were competing for U.S. consumer mindshare and wallet-share.[4] In 2011 the U.S. Treasury & Tax Bureau (TTB) approved 120,000 new certificates of label approval, dramatically increasing the number of wines that could be sold.[5]

Despite the explosion of brands and labels, chances are that a bottle of wine purchased anywhere in the U.S. came from one of only 30 companies. In fact, 82% of all shipments come from the ten largest wine companies.[6] By creating new competitively-priced brands large producers and multi-nationals drive market share, leverage economies of scale, and gain distribution clout that small artisan wineries cannot hope to match.

The Stonebridge Research Group has noted that in the past 20 years the number of U.S. distributors has declined from roughly 7,000 to 700. That means over 250,000 wines are seeking representation by only 700 distributors, who sell to roughly 143,864 retail stores and 287,286 restaurants, hotels, and other on-premises sales outlets.[7] The challenge is overwhelming for everyone – distributors, retailers, and producers.

To profitably manage this challenge nearly every distributor has tended to concentrate on large producers who can afford aggressive marketing, ad buying, and promotional discounting, as well as flood the channels with low-priced wines. This has meant reducing inventory of, or eliminating altogether, the brands of small artisan producers that cannot afford significant marketing and pricing support. This distribution environment is not unique to the U.S.

New Zealand is a robust environment for examining the most challenging issues addressed in this book. You might say it is the proverbial canary in the coal mine when it comes to early warnings of commercial danger for artisan winemakers. New Zealand is responsible for less than 1% of the global production of wine yet it enjoys a diverse geology, geography, and climate that enable cultivation of almost all grape varieties. The true marine climate and latitude range (34 to 46 degrees south) means that this small nation of 4.4 million people has the *potential* advantage of producing fine wines of unusual elegance, finesse, and character.

Offsetting this distinctive product advantage, however, is a cost structure that is burdened with relatively high land, labor, and capital costs, and significant distance from even the closest export market in Australia. Consequently, aiming at the high volume, low-cost end of the market, is not a sustainable or economically viable option. Rather, the much smaller ultra-premium end of the market is the best fit for New Zealand's fine artisan wines.

At the time of writing, nearly half of New Zealand's wine industry is owned by foreign corporations. Consequently, many important decisions that impact the future of the New Zealand wine industry are being made in New York, Paris, and Victoria, rather than in Auckland, Wellington, and Blenheim. Bulk wine has become a major component of New Zealand's product portfolio and export prices per liter have steadily declined over the past three years. Artisan winemakers and large global producers face-off against each other on a regular basis in domestic markets, board rooms, and industry meetings. Consequently, New Zealand has become a social and economic Petri dish for examining tensions between two opposing forces in the modern wine industry: Small artisan winemakers and large, multi-national, mass producers of alcoholic beverages made from fermented grape juice.

The tedium of repeating the phrase "an alcoholic beverage made from fermented grape juice" each time we spoke about the distinction between fine wine and mass-produced factory wine provoked us to coin the word "Grape-a-hol," which we use throughout this book and light-heartedly define as follows:

> **Grāpe·a·hol** [greyp-uh-haul] *noun.* alcoholic beverage made from fermented grape juice and passed off as a substitute for fine wine. *Origin.* 2012, from grape + ethyl alcohol.

Our intention was to create a new term that is an honest and unpretentious description of a very large consumer product category that we believe is fundamentally different from the fine wine product category. Over the past several decades, the line between these two categories has become blurred. Using the same term to describe both diminishes the cachet of fine wine while simultaneously providing a quality halo to factory producers who are more focused on the economics of wine-making than the art of winemaking.

Although each essay in this book stands on its own, we have arranged the chapters in an order that addresses the nature and scope of the problem, the consequences for consumers, the players who impact the future of fine wine, and three key issues (social responsibility, the environment, and language) that influence industry practices.

Finally, we would like to be clear about what *we* mean when we refer to "fine wine" and "fine artisan wine." We believe a fine wine meets *all* of the following criteria:

- It is free from standard wine faults.
- It comes from a specific wine region.
- It shows balance, length, and complexity.
- It is acknowledged by several independent and qualified sources as being of very high quality.
- It carries a significant price premium as a result of its relative scarcity and higher unit cost of production.

Furthermore, we believe a fine artisan wine also meets the following criteria:

- It can be traced to a single estate or vineyard.
- It comes from a small business producing less than 10,000 cases annually and perhaps as little as a few hundred cases of a particular wine.
- The owner/winemaker is personally involved in the winemaking process.

Gil Gardner presents a good discussion of the definition of a fine artisan wine in "How to Find the Artisan Winemakers" on Vinnobles Wine Blog.[8]

In our view, fine artisan wines cannot be judged solely on their technical merit. They also must be judged relative to their context. Is the environment in which the grapes were grown conducive to the performance of that variety? Is there a clear winemaking style or objective that guided grape growing, vinification, and market positioning? Does the team directly involved in growing the grapes and making the wine possess the knowledge, skills, abilities, and dedication consistent with a high standard of craftsmanship?

In short, a fine artisan wine is a fine wine made by a true artisan.

INTRODUCTION

Mad as Hell

In 1977, the American film *Network* won four Academy Awards. The central character of the film was Howard Beale (played by Peter Finch), the veteran anchor of an evening news program. When he learns the show is being canceled because of declining ratings, he announces on live television that he will commit suicide during the next broadcast. When he later apologizes, the network allows him to return for a respectable televised farewell.

Beale's farewell, however, turns into a heated rant about victimization that so strongly registers with the audience that ratings skyrocket and the network decides to keep him on the air as a prophet who can speak to the masses. During one of his shows, Beale incites the entire nation to throw open their windows and shout, "I'm as mad as hell, and I'm not going to take this anymore!" His television audience does precisely that and this chant of frustration rings out across the nation. The galvanizing effect on the populace catapults him to the status of a prophet and the show becomes phenomenally successful, with live audiences chanting, "We're as mad as hell, and we're not going to take this anymore."

We don't imagine ourselves as contemporary Howard Beales, inciting artisan winemakers and wine enthusiasts to march en masse to our chant. However, we do hope this book will help galvanize artisan producers and serious enthusiasts to stand up and challenge the hijacking of a 6,000-year-old craft that is being sacrificed at the altar of corporate profits.

For those of you who remember *Network*, no, we haven't forgotten that Beale was "martyred" by vested corporate interests. Regardless, the objective of this book is to expose some of the false claims, misconceptions, myths, dogma, and questionable business practices that

1

permeate the wine industry. This cannot be accomplished without sacrificing a few sacred cows, making some politically incorrect observations, and agitating some industry insiders and apologists.

"We're as mad as hell and we're not going to take it anymore!"

While these essays may irritate some in the wine industry, that is not our intent. Rather, our purpose is to communicate the perspectives of many small, artisan winemakers, whose viewpoints are rarely acknowledged openly. We anticipate that some insiders will claim we are biased and self-interested - and they will be right. But, that does not make us wrong.

We are artisan winemakers. We are proud of what we do. We spend too much money making too little product to ever achieve financial fortune and glory - at least in our lifetimes.

To us and many other people, wine is a fascinating beverage. It engages all of our senses. Each person experiences it differently. If the intention is to lubricate the mouth while eating or to lower inhibitions in a social gathering, then almost anything palatable will do. However, if the intention is to enhance a meal or a special occasion, or occupy a prominent place in a conversation, then the wine quality standard that must be achieved is much higher. The wine must be worthy of the expectations and inquisitiveness of the people consuming it.

Artisan winemakers are dedicated to making small quantities of fine wine intended to meet those higher standards. They also understand that their customers expect more than good wine paired with glib marketing pitches, flowery label descriptions, or flash advertising. Their customers want the authentic story behind the wine. They want to know where the grapes were grown, how the wine was made, and who did all the work. The simple truth is that people enjoy things made for them by other people who care deeply about what they are doing, take extra time to do it well, and are highly skilled at what they do. There is apple pie and then there is "Grandma's Apple Pie." Knowing who made it and something about the dedication, skill, and attention to detail that went into making it heightens both the anticipation and the pleasure of consuming it.

In this respect, artisan winemakers are perfectly aligned with their customers. They have immense pride in what they do, they invest considerable time and effort in their craft, and they derive great pleasure from sharing their story with their customers. For artisan winemakers, it is not just about business. It is personal.

We believe it is time for artisan winemakers and enthusiasts to speak up about the abduction of the fine wine category by profiteers, marketing shills, and corrupt distributors who hold small artisan producers hostage to terms of trade that would make loan sharks cringe.

Fortunately, information sharing is being reinvented and democratized via online blogs and social media. The ability of beverage conglomerates to control the narrative through marketing muscle and advertising dollars is diminishing. Social media and word-of-mouth are fast becoming the dominant currency of message credibility. These mediums are giving renewed life to artisan winemakers, despite a parochial wine distribution network that has typically favored larger producers who can generate demand through broad-based marketing campaigns or deep promotional discounting. The 2011 *Decanter* magazine "Power List" of the 50 people/organizations/groups with the greatest potential to move markets included amateur wine bloggers and Gary Vaynerchuk, who introduced internet video to wine blogging.

Times have changed and small wine producers are demanding more visibility. Big beverage conglomerates and global distribution networks are finding it harder to drown out the stories of the small artisan winemakers who deliver the quality and diversity that fine wine enthusiasts increasingly desire.

CHAPTER 1

140 Million Bath Tubs

Every year the world produces more than 28 billion liters of wine. That's enough to fill about 140 million average-sized bath tubs. The world is drowning in surpluses of this product. Technically it's wine, but in reality most of it is better described by the term Grape-a-hol: An alcoholic beverage made from fermented grape juice.

According to the 2010 Gomberg-Fredrikson annual wine review, ten companies account for 82% of U.S. domestic wine shipments.[1] Grape variety, vintage, place of origin, and sorting fruit for quality is largely irrelevant when pushing millions of cases of wine into a mass market. High-volume machine harvesting, factory fermentation of massive quantities, and purchases of surplus product that fails to meet the standards of quality wineries are important to the Grape-a-hol business model. Not surprisingly, labels, advertising hype, shelf space, relative pricing, volume, and manipulation of the distribution system are paramount. But there is no art, no passion, and no appreciation of what's possible.

This point was further reinforced by a story that appeared in *Decanter* on February 1, 2012, announcing the closing of *Quarterly Review of Wines* after 35 years of business. "There were many reasons for closing *Quarterly Review of Wines*, Richard L. Elia said, but chief among them was that 'passion is spent.'" The article continues:

> In a 1200-word obituary for a vanishing world, Elia blames everything from restaurant music and wine toys to corporate wine and the 100-point scale for the demise of the Winchester, Massachusetts journal.
>
> Beyond the usual explanations – upcoming retirements, the magazine world is in perilous shape, advertising is down, the digital age is king,

out-of-state wine delivery problems – what initially attracted us to wine was the romance of it,' Elia writes.

But, he said, 'Today, wine is often dominated by marketing and finance people, who measure their interest by numbers.'

Wine, he laments, is no longer made by purple-handed champions of the vineyard, but 'corporately owned wineries – some of whom are entrepreneurs or investors playing wine barons – offer(ing) intimations that wine is made in the marketplace. Now Numbers make the wine.'[2]

Inexpensive factory wine is not a new phenomenon. It has been with us for centuries. In this century and the last, a host of unpretentious and honest brands like Thunderbird, Night Train, and Hearty Burgundy made "plonk" wine famous and added the word "wino" to our vocabulary. Today, these frat-house and skid-row favorites are being swamped by a tsunami of bulk and cheap Grape-a-hol astonishingly marketed as "fine wine" and released with one goal: To sell more plonk than the other plonk peddlers.

Two competing forces – artisan winemakers and producers of factory wine – have diametrically opposed views on what constitutes fine wine vs. its commodity cousin, Grape-a-hol.

Grape-a-hol, in some instances, is cheaper than a decent beer, ready-to-drink (RTD) beverages, specialty sodas, and even branded bottled waters. In fact, it's often cheaper than the packaging - bottle, label and closure - that it comes in.

Only a tiny fraction of the world's wine is made by artisan producers. Most of us grow grapes and make wine in relative obscurity. We spend more than we should and make less than we can to pursue an ancient craft with a noble objective - to delight other people. As a group we are fiercely independent, strong-willed, deeply committed, and live at the messy intersection of art and insanity. We perceive our role essentially as muses who give voice to the land and a soul to a drink that reflects the passion of creation. Profit is a theoretical concept to us and only has meaning in the context of future generations.

Lest you think expensive artisan wines are a money pump for owners, consider this apocryphal anecdote about profit in the wine business. The patriarch of the Rothschild family was once asked by a reporter at a press conference if it was possible to make a profit in the wine business. He responded by saying "Absolutely," and then added, "it's the first 200 years that are the problem." Most artisans understand this reality all too well. Yet, despite the daunting financial obstacles they face, many feel powerless to resist the emotional grip that grape growing and wine-making has on their life. This is not a pursuit for the faint of heart or the thin of wallet.

This is why we firmly believe that artisan winemakers are the best guardians of the ancient craft of winemaking. They are an endangered species. They are also a thorn in the side of the large factory producers of Grape-a-hol.

The Great Wine War

In the late 1800s, the Western United States was in the grip of range wars – violent battles between sheepherders and cattle ranchers. The rivalry was over control of open grazing land. Cattle ranchers charged that herds of sheep over-grazed the land, leaving little or nothing for cat-tle. Sheepherders maintained that the sheep's sharp hooves aerated the soil and, with good land management, sheep and cattle could share the public lands at the center of the struggle.

The cattle ranchers had bigger herds and were better equipped with guns, horses, and money to buy political influence and local law enforcement. What ensued were acrimonious and often bloody con-frontations, including clubbing, shooting, dynamiting, poisoning, burning, and stampeding of sheep over cliffs. Thousands of sheep were killed. Farms were bankrupted. Market prices for both cattle and sheep gyrated unpredictably.

A similar version of this conflict is playing out in the global wine indus-try today. Two competing forces – artisan winemakers and producers of factory wine – have diametrically opposed views on what constitutes fine wine vs. its commodity cousin, Grape-a-hol.

Artisans seek to leverage soil, site, climate, and winemaking expertise into premium quality fine wines sold to discriminating purchasers. Com-modity producers prize brand recognition over product quality. To them, it is a battle for market share fueled by economies of scale and sales volume. This business model requires them to apply mass-production techniques in field and factory to cost-effectively increase yield and out-put, converting Nature's rewards into alcoholic beverages that can com-pete with beer and RTD brews. Unfortunately, the low-priced beverage they offer bargain hunters, while generating a profit, is driving down con-sumer expectations of how quality wine should taste.

" . . . and stay out!"

Low-volume artisan wineries offering consumers a different wine experience and a compelling story generally find they are out-gunned by the
financial and staff resources of the large corporate producers and
squeezed – if not drop-kicked – out of markets. The likelihood that these
two opposing forces can successfully co-exist in the same fine wine
product category is remote. The range wars of Western U.S. legend
finally ended with land surveys and barbed-wire fencing, backed by government regulation and law enforcement. Separating the fate of artisan
winemakers from factory producers is not that simple.

Few governments are prepared to enter the fray for fear of a political
backlash from vested interests and well-funded lobbyists. Many regulations, like the three-tier distribution structure in the U.S., are contemporary barbed-wire fences that constrain interstate commerce in an
effort to shield local state distributors and retailers from winery direct
sales. These regulations favor big producers who have a vice-like grip on
those same distributors, putting consumers and smaller artisan wineries
at a disadvantage with higher cost and reduced access. Even regulations
protecting geographical identifications (appellations) languish in com-
mittees or are slow to be implemented because they might limit the flex-
ibility of producers who liberally, and sometimes deceptively, use the
names of highly regarded wine regions to help sell lesser products that
otherwise might never make it to the consumer's shopping cart.

The real tragedy is that the marketing campaigns of factory producers have taken control of the fine wine narrative. Small, artisan producers have suffered in silence while corporate giants dominate the wine distribution system, dictate public choice by controlling shelf space, buy visibility, and mislead consumers with a sales proposition that offers something for nearly nothing.

The strangle-hold that large factory producers have on the global distribution system has impeded meaningful challenges from all but those with the deepest pockets. However, there are signs that their grip on consumer perceptions may be slipping. As noted earlier, word-of-mouth via social media is an increasingly viable and influential channel for consumers, professionals, and enthusiasts to communicate with each other. Reviewers in newspapers and specialty magazines are no longer the only power brokers that can make or break reputations. The blogosphere has expanded and redefined the space within which opinion is framed.

Perhaps most encouragingly, young consumers are increasingly educating themselves about wines and the stories behind them. This is an Achilles heel for many big producers. When you peel away the hyperbole and flash advertising, the stories behind these mass-market wines sound trivial and often no more exciting than reading a bank statement. Young consumers appear to be demanding greater visibility with regard to the origins of the product they purchase and drink for pleasure and are unforgiving to those who would deceive and mislead them.

Make no mistake – there is nothing wrong or immoral about inexpensive, good quality, Grape-a-hol as long as it's not represented as something that it is not. And, while the days of the Grape-a-hol manufacturers are far from over, the days of their masquerading in fine-wine clothing may be coming to an end. Like the tailors in Hans Christian Anderson's *The Emperor's New Clothes*, their fakery ultimately will be exposed by those unfettered by complicity.

CHAPTER 2

Truth-Telling from Corporate Wine Closets

In April 2010, Michael Mondavi openly rattled the cages of corporate wine producers by bluntly declaring at the Fine Wine 2010 conference in Ribera del Duero that big corporations are not capable of success in the fine wine market. He was quoted in the *Harpers Wine & Spirit Trades Review* as saying:

> "When big corporations enter, those brands lose their passion, those brands lose their style. The chief financial officer starts making wine-making decisions" . . .
>
> "I had the partial luxury of running a publicly-owned company (Robert Mondavi) for 11 years. The ability to ask the question 'how do I make better wines – what's the right thing to do?' evaporates.
>
> "You start talking to the chief financial officer and ask the question 'how do I improve earnings?' not 'how do I make better wines?', 'how do I improve the return on assets?', not 'how do I establish a better quality vineyard for 10 or 20 years from now?' . . .[1]

Responses to the piece were mixed, but most supported his position.

The over-riding focus of executives in publicly-traded wine companies is: Creative marketing, not creative winemaking; artistic branding, not artistic blending. Mondavi noted in the same speech that "the questions that CEOs are forced to ask are quite different to the questions that independent proprietors take in running their own businesses. Wines in the consumer product arena are ideal for corporate ownership, but when you move from that style of wine to fine wine it's passion and dedication that's needed."

Clearly, independent proprietors have financial considerations that influ-ence their decisions as well. The difference, however, may be that the artisan producer of fine wines sees quality as a concrete manifestation of a very personal vision. Each vintage is a reflection of the artisan's success or failure in achieving that vision. Every year the outcome is personal. And every year the owner is emotionally invested in repeating and exceeding each success, as much for personal validation as for financial remuneration. We believe this is the source of the "passion to succeed" that Mondavi attributes to independent and family wineries.

"Start using oak flavoring instead of those expensive French barrels."

A few years ago we were having dinner with a well-known winemaker from a medium-sized producer who had been acquired by one the largest wine corporations in the world. During the course of the evening we talked about life before and after the deal. We were curious how the company culture had changed since the acquisition.

As former consultants in this area and authors of a popular book on mergers & acquisitions and accelerating transitions, we are all too familiar with the fallout from financially-driven growth plans that lead companies to gobble up smaller players, often riding roughshod over the very people and processes that attracted the acquirer in the first place.

When we asked the question directly, the winemaker summarized the impact more eloquently than we ever could. "Before we were acquired, we were always looking for ways to earn a dollar more for our wines," he said. "And after the deal was done, everything switched to how could we save ten cents on making the wine."

For both winemakers and consumers, there is nothing encouraging about that all-too-common answer. When a larger corporation takes over a smaller winery, short-sighted financial and brand management is quickly applied and devolves to the lowest common denominator. Decades of work spent building a quality artisan brand can be undermined in a matter of months.

You might call this the Procrustean strategy of winery acquisition. In Greek mythology, Procrustes, a son of Poseidon, would invite travelers to Athens to spend the night in his home. He had an iron bed and insisted that all travelers fit the bed. To accomplish this, he cut off the feet or head of anyone too tall for the bed and stretched anyone too short. In all cases, his visitors died.

One factory winemaker candidly admitted that he gets paid to produce volume. If the wine turns out to be balanced and flavorful, that's a serendipitous accident for which he's happy to take the credit.

Many large corporate acquirers of artisan vineyards appear to be applying the same template. They stubbornly adhere to low-cost and low-price models that ignore differentiators like quality and distinctiveness that might legitimately deliver price premiums and growth in sales volume. Instead they ride the commodity-product slide until sales drop off and then repackage their product under another market-tested label for another run. Their primary objective is to produce commodity quality consistent with the lowest possible cost.

Many years ago, Steve Martin, then an aspiring young comic, joked about making money by writing a book titled *How to Turn a Million in Real Estate into Fifty Bucks Cash.* This mock "how-to" book could have served as the guide for even the most sophisticated Grape-a-hol manufacturers who undermine their own strategies for growth and profitability by following an uninspired and simplistic business model.

Somewhere along the way to executive bonuses, they lose sight of the fact that a 1% increase in revenue while holding cost at current levels will drive more to the bottom line than a 1% reduction in expense. It's basic arithmetic. But then again, when you have a surplus of Grape-a-hol the fastest and surest way to reduce inventory is to reduce price.

Were this myopic focus on cost reduction confined to only these corporate financial engineers it would not be a big issue. However, the waves these behemoths make in the global ocean of wine are so big that other producers are virtually forced to follow in their cost-driven, price-reducing wake for fear of being swamped by backwash if they pursue a more thoughtful course.

The factory producers seem not to have learned the lessons ecologists have tried to teach us about manipulating an ecosystem. Changing just one or two things can have negative cascading effects. Consider the following example from Michael Mauboussin's book, *Think Twice*.[2]

When Yellowstone Park's population of wild game – elk, antelope and deer – was being depleted by hunters and poachers in the late 1800s, the U.S. Cavalry was given responsibility for the park, including rebuilding the wild game population. A few years of special protection and feeding led to rapid increases in the deer and elk population, which proceeded to over-graze the region and deplete flora, causing extensive soil erosion, damage to streams, and reduction in trout spawning.

In the winter of 1919/20, when 60% of the elk population starved to death due to over-grazing, the National Park Service assumed the cause was predators and began killing wolves, mountain lions, and coyotes. This only made the situation worse, as now there were no natural predators to reduce the over-population of wild game and the over-grazing. The predators had to be reintroduced by the mid-1990s.

This story is not so different from what is being perpetrated in the wine industry by corporate producers who attempt to reduce grape cost per metric ton by increasing yield. There are only a few immutable laws of winemaking. One of them is the relationship between yield, quality, and cost. The fewer the grapes you load up on a vine, the higher the quality will be of those that you harvest – and the higher your ultimate cost per liter of wine.

On the other hand, if you minimize pruning and mechanically harvest both first and second sets, you increase yield, lower your cost per unit, and reduce the quality of the crop. Carry that mindset into the winery and through the winemaking process and you further reduce cost and quality. The resulting surplus drives prices further down, narrowing profit margins, forcing more price cutting, further decreasing the quality of wine in the market and, in the process, training consumers to look for and develop a taste for an inferior product.

Economists have consistently demonstrated that in the absence of price competition, for example in regulated markets with price floors, product quality improves because products are differentiated on the basis of quality – not price. As long as corporate wine producers compete primarily on price and market manipulation – for example by labeling their Grape-a-hol as "fine wine" – and as long as they rely on cost-cutting to manage their margins, the average consumer will not experience wine that has achieved its full potential at the hands of skilled artisan winemakers, who cannot survive trying to compete on price alone.

During a less than sober moment at a recent vineyard and winery conference in California, one factory winemaker candidly admitted that he gets paid to produce volume. If the wine turns out to be balanced and flavorful, that's a serendipitous accident for which he's happy to take the credit. His true objective is to make a sufficiently palatable alcoholic beverage for washing down food. It seemed patently clear to him that price trumps flavor in the marketplace: Passable wine at a low price is a good deal for the consumer and profitable for his company.

In his school of thought, consumers can get used to anything from grape soda to mouthwash. If there is smart, store-level marketing and an attractive label reinforcing the perception that his table wine is fine wine, average purchasers will align their expectations with the belief that this is what fine wine tastes like and they have discovered a genuine bargain. Psychologists have a name for this: Confirmation Bias. Apparently, the company of the winemaker in question has an entire marketing and branding team dedicated to lowering consumers' expectations of fine wine and what it should cost.

Did he feel any remorse over this deception? Yes.

Was he prepared to do anything about it? No.

Why? Nearly everyone participating in the conversation that evening agreed that whatever obligation they might feel to consumers, these were the new economics of wine.

The bottom line is that you get what you pay for - with one major exception. The less you pay, proportionally, the less quality you get. From the standpoint of value and quality, the worst consumer wine deals on the planet are on the cheapest bottles of wine, unless of course you are just looking for a cheap buzz.

CHAPTER 3

The Plonk That Launched a Thousand Ships

Conflict makes good theatre. It's especially entertaining when the combatants are industry giants taking opposite sides of a quality controversy that just will not go away.

The front page of a California newspaper read: "Wine Industry Titans Dispute Merits of Tanker Shipments."[1] The story focused on a simmering debate that erupted between two players who were able to move markets. The CEO for the proposition enthusiastically asserted that:

> "By transporting by ship (in tanks), the wine is less exposed to the air than it would be in bottles or barrels, and the gentle rolling of the sea is far better for it than the harsh jolting it receives in the bottle during land transport."

The CEO opposed to the proposition emphatically insisted that his company would:

> " . . . continue bottling and sealing its products at the winery to protect wine quality, rather than avail itself of lower freight costs obtainable by ocean tanker shipment." He added that their investigations concluded that the quality of wine "could not be protected under the conditions imposed by such transportation, including the hazards of carrying varied cargoes in the wine tanks on return voyages."

This headline could well have appeared in a contemporary wine industry publication, but it didn't. This "theatrical production" appeared in the *Lodi News Sentinel* on October 10, 1957 - 55 years ago. The antagonists were, respectively, Louis Petri, president of United Vintners, Inc. and

Ernest Gallo, co-owner of E. & J. Gallo Winery. Petri marketed his 22,000 ton floating wine cellar outfitted with steel tanks as improving the wine by harnessing the "gentle rolling of the sea." Gallo on the other hand was convinced that Petri's contraption was actually damaging wine quality.

Why do we refer to this episode as a theatrical production? The protagonists were the two largest wine producers in the United States. Their product was vin ordinaire - jug wine, not ordinarily praised for quality.[2] In fact, arguably few people would detect any difference in quality between their products - if indeed there was any. Yet, quality was at the core of the marketing battle. And, given the risks of contamination, the economic argument reinforcing bulk shipping was specious. But this was only the beginning.

If you are in the business of making large volumes of Grape-a-hol and getting it to thirsty, non-discriminating consumers around the world who want cheap wine, there really is no better option.

Today, the most common way to move large volumes of Grape-a-hol around the world - especially on ships - is a 24,000 liter plastic bladder or Containerpac that fits neatly inside a 20 foot steel container.[3] The manufacturers of these marvelous inventions also make bladders for bulk shipping drinking water, fruit juice, beer, olive oil, mineral oil, palm oil, castor oil, fuel oil, bio-diesel, and who knows what else. Those who have concerns about the impact this method of shipment has on the quality of wine might want to read the wine quality report prepared by the Waste & Resources Action Program (WRAP), an organization that "helps individuals businesses and local authorities to reduce waste and recycle more, making better use of resources and helping to tackle climate change."[4] The argument in favor of this shipping method cites the following advantages:

- Greater thermal inertia in shipment (less likely for temperature to fluctuate).

- Cost-effective - the same container that would include 10,584 liters in bottles would hold 24,000 liters in a bag - thereby lowering the unit cost of transport.

- Marketing and packaging options close to the point of sale to meet consumer preferences.

- Reduced damage to packaging (e.g., label scuffing).

Of course there are some potential drawbacks:

- Possible contamination from previous cargo or fumigation chemicals.

- Oxidation.

- Re-fermentation (for sweet or non-sterile filtered wines).

- Not practical for small volumes of premium wines.

If you are in the business of making large volumes of Grape-a-hol and getting it to thirsty, non-discriminating consumers around the world who want cheap wine, there really is no better option . . . unless you lack the courage to take *the next bold step.*

The next bold step is the most cost-effective, efficient, and environmentally friendly method of delivering Grape-a-hol to the non-discriminating masses. Wine is 85%–87% H_2O and 12%–14% ethyl alcohol. These are commodities easily available at very low cost in virtually every wine-consuming market. So, from an environmental perspective, 99% of the mass that is shipped in these bladders is moving two fluids around the world that already are available at the destination point! The only "unique" component is the less than 1% of "grapey bits." Imagine being able to concentrate and ship those "bits" in tablet form and then re-hydrate and add 105ml of ethyl alcohol at the point of sale!

Now that is an idea that will have real impact on carbon footprint and the cost of shipping. A whole shipping container worth of wine in a small DHL overnight package! That would warm the heart of every Grape-a-hol distributor.

If you really wanted to complete the illusion, you would sell the tablets to consumers in foil packs that could be peeled apart and applied to a reusable bottle as the front and back bottle labels. Drop in a tablet, fill to the water-level line, add the pre-measured ampoule of ethyl alcohol, tighten the screw cap, give it a few shakes and pop it into the fridge. Thirty minutes later you have authentic Marlborough Sauvignon Blanc complete with a genuine brand label! The power to create a miracle and turn water into wine would be within the grasp of every consumer.

"Plop, plop, fizz, fizz. Oh how easy it is!"

But . . . would it taste like New Zealand Sauvignon Blanc? Does it really matter? Most of the Sauvignon Blanc shipped in bulk to the U.K., Germany, the U.S., Australia, and China bears little resemblance to the delicate and aromatically distinctive wine that originally made it so attractive. This environmentally conscientious, consumer friendly, cost-effective, highly flexible adult beverage solution could lead to a revolution in "wine" drinking, especially among the new generation of wine consumers already being taught to accept Grape-a-hol as the new normal.

Granted, most people would consider such a scenario just plain silly. After all, who would drink wine that was made from a tablet? That would be almost as ridiculous as drinking orange juice or milk made from powder.

Or is it?

Kraft Foods' Tang powdered orange drink is classified as one of Kraft's power brands with sales exceeding U.S. $1 billion annually.[5] The 2011 global forecast for exported milk powder is 3.3 million metric tons.[6] Why not wine?

It doesn't take a soothsayer, quantum physicist, or clairvoyant to see where the bulk wine market is going, or why the current container of choice is a 24,000 liter bag inside a banged-up steel shipping container. The gap between Grape-a-hol and fine artisan wines is widening every day. The creation of mock wine is only a few steps removed from the current state-of-the-art mass-market "wine."

The days of buying the components and mixing them in your own kitchen may not be that far away. Will it taste good and get you drunk? Absolutely. Will it be wine? Well, that is debatable.

The ingredients of Tang include sugar, citric acid, natural and artificial flavor, ascorbic acid (vitamin C), maltodextrin, calcium phosphate, guar and xanthan gums, sodium acid pyrophosphate, artificial color, yellow 5, yellow 6, BHA. Is it orange juice? Even Kraft Foods calls it an orange "drink."

It reminds us of when some friends visited California from Iowa. As a special treat we took them to the world-famous Buena Vista Café in San Francisco for a Buena Vista Irish Coffee – a special concoction created in 1952 of coffee, sugar, Irish whisky, and cream. After downing the drink, Stella said "That was wonderful – do you suppose I could make it from instant coffee, bourbon, and Dream Whip?"

"Sure you could," was the response. "But it wouldn't be Irish Coffee."

Does bulk wine (the precursor to wine tablets) taste like real wine? Of course it does – especially to the non-discriminating drinker. But, as many would point out, it is, at best, "a distant cousin."

CHAPTER 4

The Mouse That Tried to Roar

In 1955 the Irish-American writer Leonard Wibberley published a satirical novel entitled *The Mouse That Roared.* The story was about an imaginary country in Europe called the Duchy of Grand Fenwick. Supposedly located in the Alps between Switzerland and France, the tiny country (3 miles by 5 miles) proudly retained a pre-industrial economy dependent almost entirely on making a wine called Pinot Grand Fenwick. However, an American winery starts to make a knockoff version called "Pinot Grand Enwick," thereby putting the Duchy on the verge of bankruptcy.

After considerable discussion, the Prime Minister decides that their only course of action is to declare war on the United States. Anticipating a quick defeat (their army is very small and only possesses bows and arrows), the country confidently expects to rebuild itself through the generous foreign aid that the U.S. bestows on all its vanquished enemies – as it did for Germany and Japan at the end of World War II.
Through a series of bizarre events, the tiny country's plan for a swift defeat is foiled and instead it ends up capturing a dreaded doomsday machine from the U.S., thus shifting the global balance of power to a group of nations called the "Tiny Twenty" who pressure the superpowers of the world into peaceful obedience.

Considering the rapid rise in bulk wine exports from New Zealand over the past several years, one wonders if *this* tiny nation's wine business strategy is to create a 21st century sequel to that classic comedy by effectively declaring unwinnable economic war on the bulk wine superpowers of the world.

"Isn't that cute! A tiny "bulk" mouse."

Transition from Wine Surplus Relief Valve to Modus Operandi

Historically, New Zealand has not been a player in the bulk wine market. Costs of production, volume, and quality considerations rendered that route to market economically barren. Up until 2008 bulk wine sales from NZ hovered around 5% and merely provided a means of dumping surplus into the bulk market rather than down the drain. It was not an economically viable solution at the industry level.

In 2008, a series of vintage and economic factors conspired to drive ever increasing volumes through this dubious route to market. Shipment of bulk sales quadrupled and then surpassed 30% in 2010. In some months, bulk exports have approached 50% (see graph),[1] placing New Zealand in the unenviable position of following in the footsteps of their Australian neighbors, albeit without the scale to back it up.

With the 15% increase over forecast in the 2011 vintage, and reports that there are no capacity problems, it is likely that bulk wine numbers will continue to rise. Instead of addressing this strategically, the leaders of New Zealand Winegrowers, the national organization for the sector, in what can only be described as an attempt to lower expectations, is telling its members to brace themselves for the new reality of bulk wine being a major component of export shipments.

New Zealand Bulk Wine as a Percent of Total Exports

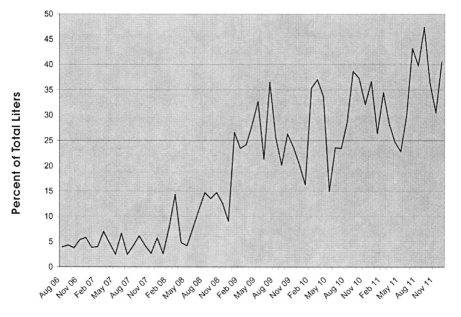

Time Period

It is true that New Zealand earns the highest price per liter for wine imported into the U.K. However, being the price leader for the low-cost wine segment is a dubious distinction. That reputation may evaporate with the predictable rise in bulk sales as a result of the strong 2011 vintage.

The Bulk Wine Conundrum

In addition to the risk of price deterioration from flooding an important market like the U.K. with bulk product, there also is a serious threat to quality from handling wine in an unpackaged format. For example, aromatics are a significant component in the enjoyment of quality wine. Sauvignon Blanc, New Zealand's largest wine export by volume (nearly 84% in 2011), is aromatically fragile. Extensive handling, temperature fluctuations and inadvertent exposure to oxygen degrades the aromatics and lowers quality.

These economic and quality issues surrounding bulk shipment have created a real conundrum for the New Zealand wine industry.[2] The pieces of this puzzle add up to a scenario that would be comical if it were not so serious:

1. Domestic taxation policy on wine does not differentiate between fine wine and Grape-a-hol. The volume-based excise tax imposed at the point of production, rather than the point of sale, means that producers retain a much bigger margin by exporting inexpensive wine than releasing it on the domestic market.

2. A recently published study by the New Zealand Ministry of Agriculture and Forestry has demonstrated that growers producing lower yield and presumably higher quality Sauvignon Blanc grapes earned no more per metric ton than those loading up the vines and aiming at the bulk market.[3] This removes the incentive to make high-quality wine.

3. The savings from shipping wine in bulk are enticing winemakers to become volume producers at the lowest possible manufacturing cost.

These trends have combined to accelerate exports of non-packaged product and led industry leaders to proclaim that bulk is the new reality for New Zealand wine production. However, two critical factors make this a flawed declaration: The industry's high cost structure and its limited production capacity. The majority of New Zealand wineries are unable to scale up to compete profitably as low-cost producers in the global wine market.

At the industry's 2011 Romeo Bragato conference, one presenter audaciously suggested that New Zealand's biggest challenge was to achieve greater scale. Given New Zealand's capacity limitations, this is like telling a short person they need to be taller. At the same conference, a wine-market analyst from Rabobank bluntly pointed out that few, if any, New Zealand producers had a clear understanding of their true cost of goods sold.

There are few consequences of business decisions that are more devastating in impact or lasting in effect than consumer disappointment with a previously well-regarded brand.

To suggest that the new production reality for the New Zealand wine industry is to increase volume and lower cost to support shipment of bulk wine is pure strategic folly.

Ultimately, New Zealand's last and best line of defense against downward price pressure is the provenance, quality, and environmental sensitivity of its exported products. These valuable product attributes resonate with customers across all segments, except those feeding at the bottom of the price pyramid. One can only wonder then why wine industry leadership would be so willing to risk degrading this distinctive competitive advantage by permitting it to be applied to bulk wine bottled offshore.

Undermining a Valuable Symbol

The New Zealand Winegrowers association has long promoted the importance of environmental responsibility. The Sustainable Winegrowing New Zealand (SWNZ) program is intended to bring all vineyards and wineries into compliance with sustainability standards over the next few years. SWNZ promotional activities clarify the value of the SWNZ logo as material proof that a winery and/or vineyard operates in a manner consistent with New Zealand's global reputation of being clean and green.

The problem, however, is that falling wine prices and a punitive tax structure force more wine offshore in bulk. The result is that less of it is permitted to carry the distinctive SWNZ logo because the certification program did not permit offshore bottling.

We say "did not permit" because as economic pressure to ship more wine in bulk mounted, New Zealand Winegrowers decided to change the rules and allow certification of offshore bottling plants. While some will argue that this is a strategic blunder for a country with a stated mission to focus on higher prices and premium wines, it does provide aid and comfort to those focused on the low-cost, commodity end of the market. These producers can now find cover under a valuable logo representing sustainability and an international branding campaign.

Putting aside the strategic implications of these actions, New Zealand has increased its risk of catastrophic brand damage from tampering and adulteration scandals at the hand of unscrupulous traders, brokers, offshore bottlers, or producers. For those scurrying around the cellar of the price pyramid, the temptation to "extend" or alter the volume of wine may be impossible to resist. After all, if the product already is perceived to be diminished in quality, will 10-15% dilution or substitution really matter?

Adulteration and tampering with volume has plagued the wine industry for centuries. The controls often are too weak and the motivation to cheat too great. When this is combined with jurisdictional issues, wide variations in health and safety practices, and substantial costs of enforcement, we are left with an honor system. It is easy to write rigorous standards and procedures to protect product quality, but absent the mechanism to enforce, sanction, and severely punish offenders, it is largely a toothless and theoretical exercise.

Even more problematic is the lasting and devastating impact that a highly publicized tampering or quality scandal can have on the reputation of a nation's product, even if caused by only a few disreputable producers, cut-and-run traders, or a simple manufacturing mistake. If you have any doubt, think lead-laced toys, poisoned pet food and toothpaste, and tainted milk powder from China. So devastating has this publicity been for the country's pride and reputation that many Chinese consumers now prefer products that are produced elsewhere.

Another compelling case involved Perrier's fall from its lofty perch in the bottled water market after trace amounts of benzene were discovered in a small sample of bottles.[4] If you are interested in further examples just Google "Anti-freeze in Austrian wine," "Wither Hills scandal," or "top ten wine scandals." It makes for interesting, if not disturbing, reading.

Casey Stengel, the famous New York Yankees manager, once said, "Most games are lost." He was referring to the fact that errors by the losing team were often the dominant factor in a game's outcome. For a nation like New Zealand, allowing SWNZ certification to go offshore is potentially such an error.

Consider that New Zealand is responsible for less than 1% of the global supply of wine. It holds an exalted price position in the U.K. and is dependent primarily on one variety (Sauvignon Blanc). Exposing itself to this kind of national brand risk is hard to justify, yet from the perspective of those focused on low-cost production, the economics of large-volume distribution trump national brand risk.

While it is true that New Zealand Winegrowers sets the same standards for wine bottled offshore as it does for wine bottled in New Zealand, there is one notable difference. Wine bottled in New Zealand must obtain export certification prior to shipment. Export certification includes analytical and sensory analysis that ensures minimum wine standards are met as defined by the New Zealand Food Safety Authority (NZFSA). No export certificate, no shipping. If there is anything wrong with the product, it is intercepted *before* it departs for an overseas market.

Bulk wine, on the other hand, is tested in *unpackaged* form (generally a large tank) before shipment. Once bottled offshore, it is released into the market and then sample bottles are returned to New Zealand for testing. If those samples fail to meet NZFSA standards, the only option at that point is to recall the product.

To a casual observer this might sound like a reasonable process. However, anyone involved in the production of wine knows there is considerable risk of degradation, contamination, tampering, dilution, or adulteration during the gap between placing finished wine in a tank (or container bag) and committing it to final customer packaging. Those risks multiply when the time lag covers weeks and the distance traveled is measured in thousands of miles, including crossing national boundaries which makes enforcement of standards difficult.

Added to the above risk is the diabolical practice of some unscrupulous individuals who submit false samples to cover their deceptive practices. While this reprehensible action is possible with domestically released as well as exported wine, it is much more difficult to apprehend and punish the culprits when they live on the other side of the world.

New Zealand wine that is oxidized, malodorous, or has other sensory faults – all risks of extensive handling prior to bottling – might therefore make it into important foreign markets before New Zealand authorities become aware of a problem. Only the most extreme faults are likely to trigger intervention. Product recalls are expensive public relations nightmares and companies will go to great lengths to avoid them, often rationalizing that the faults are minimal, mostly subjective, and don't involve public safety. An example of how one of these concerns might be minimized is reflected in an opinion held by some viticulturists that the qualitative difference between low-yielding and high-yielding Sauvignon Blanc grapes is not readily perceptible and therefore not a wine-quality issue in the mass market.

The risks of offshore bottling are not likely to involve public safety. However, the most troubling part of this scenario is the distinct possibility that a large volume of inferior examples of a prized national product could be masquerading around important foreign markets as authentic New Zealand wine, complete with an official SWNZ logo. There are few consequences of business decisions that are more devastating in impact or lasting in effect than consumer disappointment with a previously well-regarded brand.

With so much on the line, why would a single producer, let alone an entire national industry, willingly assume such risk to a reputation? And, if problems occur, from which corner of the industry are the abuses likely to come?

We do not believe that the product-quality problems will come from the large, multi-national wine and spirits corporations. Were they the only ones bottling offshore, there would be less cause for concern. These players carry the greatest economic risk of all if substandard products are released into important markets they serve. It is in their best interest to diligently comply with SWNZ standards and protect the integrity of the distinctive logo. However, what is exponentially more difficult to control is brand damage caused by brokers and traders who are moving large volumes as part of commodity transactions. Like short sellers in the stock market, their only motivation is to capture margin opportunity. Preserving brand value is not on the arbitrageur's radar screen and after the damage is done they will move on to other trades, leaving the New Zealand wine industry red-faced and holding an empty bag.

Given all the drawbacks, we return again to the fundamental question: How exactly does handing SWNZ branding rights to low-cost offshore production proponents help the New Zealand wine industry focus on higher prices and the premium end of the market?

It doesn't.

In Arthur Conan Doyle's *The Adventures of Sherlock Holmes*, the master detective at one point says, "There is nothing so deceptive as an obvious fact." Consider this fact: More than 45% of the New Zealand wine industry is owned by foreign corporations and the majority of the bulk is exported by a few of the largest players in the global industry. They are not alone in this, though. Many of New Zealand's large producers are big fans of the "bag in a box," as is a small army of independent brokers and traders, especially when it comes to shipping Sauvignon Blanc at NZ$2.50–$3.50 per liter.

Whether or not those rates are economically sustainable is debatable. What is not debatable is where it positions New Zealand wine in the global market – an emerging, national Grape-a-hol manufacturer with a lifespan that might well be measured with a stopwatch. With only 33,000 hectares planted and pressure to pull rather than plant vines, this bulk wine-producing country's transition from respected producer of quality wines to loss-leading follower in the bulk wine market will make good fodder for business-school case studies on the commoditization and decline of a national brand.

The Myth of Price Recovery

An interesting rebuttal to this prediction is a simple but flawed argument that the price pendulum will swing in the other direction in a few years' time when there is a potential shortage of Sauvignon Blanc compared to forecast demand.

On December 13, 2011, a story appeared on the front page of the business section of the *New Zealand Herald* entitled "Wine about to get more expensive as glut runs out." Citing the results of an independent strategic study of the New Zealand wine industry completed by PricewaterhouseCoopers, the article stated: "The outlook was for the balance between supply and demand to tighten, which should lead to higher prices. The sales potential for wine by 2021 could grow by 170 million litres to reach nearly 400 million litres if unconstrained by supply." New Zealand Winegrowers' chief executive Philip Gregan noted, "I think that when you look at the numbers in the report the days are starting to be numbered for those cut price deals." However, the article also stated that, "The outlook for higher wine prices was likely to be slow to boost growers' returns due to both their weaker negotiating position and the impact of unviable growers leaving the industry."

A closer reading of the PricewaterhouseCoopers report released to members of New Zealand Winegrowers reveals a story decidedly less optimistic for producers than the *Herald*'s headline suggested.

While the forecast shortage of wine may transpire a number of years in the future, it does not naturally follow that current near-commodity prices will be abandoned in favor of prices anywhere close to previous levels.

A series of studies by the behavioral economics researchers Dan Ariely, George Lowenstein, and Drazen Prelec have demonstrated that once a price is established in a consumer's mind, it becomes an "anchor" and shapes perceptions of future prices for that product.[5] This should give pause to people who are considering lowering prices to reduce inventory levels. As a market becomes saturated with lower-priced products, the new price reality becomes the anchored norm and is likely to eliminate or constrict consumer acceptance of price increases not only for that product, but also for related products in that category. As any boat owner knows, anchors go down a lot easier than they come up, especially if they get snagged on the debris that clutters up the bottom.

A compelling example of price anchoring is the case of Chilean wines. Despite being lauded with the 2009 Silver Anvil Award of Marketing

Consumer Products Excellence by the Public Relations Society of America, Chilean wines have taken a beating in the marketplace. As reported by Russ Josephs on *The Brand Channel* on February 16, 2010:

> Foreigners are actually drinking more Chilean wine than ever, with shipments up nearly 18 percent in 2009, as opposed to California wineries, whose 2009 shipments dropped by 4 million cases, according to consulting firm Gomberg, Fredrikson & Associates.
>
> The problem is that people are choosing cheaper vintages, preventing Chile's wine brands from being able to "break out of the $10- to $20-per-bottle price point," said Bill Crowley, professor emeritus at Sonoma State University.
>
> A few years back, the Chilean wine industry decided to simultaneously curb supply and fund a global campaign aimed at promoting their wares, all in the name of achieving higher prices.
>
> But the recession destroyed this goal, and currently the industry is in something of a holding pattern. Making matters worse are the vintners who are selling in bulk to compete with countries like Argentina, Australia, and South Africa – all of whom are fighting for a share of the low-end wine trade.
>
> This means that when the recession finally lifts, the quality that Chilean wineries were hoping to embody may be tarnished.[6]

Research on price anchoring has been replicated with a range of products from wine to chocolates, books, electronic devices, and real estate. It begins to explain why research by Daniel Putler found that when the price of eggs was reduced people bought slightly more eggs. But, when the price of eggs rose, people "cut back their consumption by *two and a half times*."[7] This latter finding was also replicated with orange juice, which is priced and shipped similarly to bulk wine.

The dispiriting conclusion from all the research, examples, and case studies on price anchoring is that even world-class promotional efforts may fall on deaf ears. Marketers can position, pitch, promote, and plead with consumers until they are blue in the face, but if they are unable to counteract the effect of bulk cannibalization of a country's wine brand by Grape-a-hol producers, day traders, and commodity brokers, then all their marketing creativity will be nothing more than well-intentioned delusional thinking and a monumental waste of time.

Those holding out hope for a return to previous Sauvignon Blanc price premiums may be in for a long wait. In the meantime, economic pressure from banks, investors, and owners will continue to whittle down the number of producers dedicated to making quality wine.

And what will happen in a few years when the bulk wine channel becomes New Zealand's dominant route to global markets?

If the predictable devastation comes to pass from this unwise excursion into the economic battlefield dominated by bulk wine superpowers, even the magnitude of foreign aid anticipated by the imaginary citizens of the Duchy of Grand Fenwick will not be enough to save the New Zealand wine industry.

CHAPTER 5

Carnival Tricks

Many years ago a low-budget carnival came to town in the late summer. There were head-spinning rides, a Ferris wheel, cotton candy, cheap hot dogs, balloons, and dozens of game stalls where young men could test their skills and impress their girlfriends by winning a big, soft, stuffed panda bear or giraffe.

One weekend evening, wandering down the midway and hoping to attract the attention of cute girls, a group of boys decided their chances would be greatly improved if they were each carrying a giant stuffed animal for a deserving young lady. The problem was that they would have to win these prizes.

Most of the carnival games were rigged and "winners" were lured into repeated plays by winning tiny consolation prizes - trinkets - that could be traded in multiples for the big prize. These young Casanovas had neither the money nor the time to pursue a trading-up strategy.

Almost on cue, a carnival barker yells at the group, "Guys, I have a deal for you."

The "deal" was the famously rigged Hoop Toss game. The object was to toss a bamboo hoop over a peg and get it to fall completely around the square base. The game's operator demonstrates the simplicity of the game by casually tossing a hoop over one of several dozen pegs - it settles nicely over the base. Of course the hoops used by the barker are slightly larger than the hoops provided to contestants.

"Boys, here is the deal," he says. "You each get three attempts and if any one of you wins, I will give each of you a big stuffed animal to attract the girls!"

This offer demanded clarification. "Wait a minute," says one of the boys. "If just one of us does it we ALL get a BIG stuffed animal? Not one of those puny little plastic ducks, right?"

"That's right," says the barker. He takes one of the hoops and flicks it again over one of the pegs where it settles. "It must land completely over the base like this." He then flicks another hoop. This one lands on an angle, and he says, "Not like that." He then throws another and scores a perfect hit.

"Boys, it's been a slow night," the barker then explains. "I made all my money during the week and these stuffed animals are paid for. So I don't really care if you all win one. I just want to make a few more bucks before we close tonight."

After a brief huddle, each of the boys handed over $2. Other people were gathering to watch six local guys were about to separate a "carny" from a veritable herd of giant stuffed pandas.

The first contestant "tests" throwing techniques. One hoop got excruciatingly close, causing the gathering crowd to moan in unison. The next one was a total bust, with one hoop completely missing the table. The operator says, "Let me show you the technique again." He tosses one of the hoops in a gentle arc and it falls neatly over the base. Everybody cheers. The next victim was determined to be the hero and proclaimed victory before his first toss.

"Step aside BOYS, and let a pro show you how it is done." Three clean misses later everybody was laughing and his friends were punching him in the arm.

The crowd was building and the pressure on the remaining three was mounting, especially since a group of cute girls had wandered over to watch.

Contestant No. 4 tosses all three at the same time thinking that the laws of entropy would work in his favor. They didn't. The next hopeful tries a theoretically flawed "hula hoop" technique, hoping the spinning rings will burrow themselves onto the base.

Finally, the last young punter steps up. Feeling the weight of his friends, the girls, and the crowd on his shoulders he carefully pitches the first two hoops in majestic arcs toward the targets. Both catch the edge of the front peg and flip over, missing the mark. Everybody groans. The final toss is almost perfect, landing over the peg and settling down with only the edge of the hoop caught on one of the four corners. Everybody holds their breath, hoping a micro tremor from the earth's core would tease it over the edge. The tremor never came.

"Boys," the operator says. "I was certain you were going to do it. How about another try? I'll even give you an extra hoop each," he added.

Embarrassed and broke, the boys step back, only to be replaced by a dozen others, all with $2 in hand and eager to try their luck.

This wine marketing ploy is rigged. It has all the elements of a carnival scam, including confusing messages, misdirection, and a low-risk, something-for-almost-nothing offer.

A ploy similar to this carnival trick takes place in supermarkets and liquor stores around the world on a daily basis. Grape-a-hol purchased from discount brokers is branded with the country of origin and a label with a cute animal or pastoral image featuring the name of a non-existent but intriguing-sounding bay, cove, ridge, region, or road. It is sold to unsuspecting customers as a bargain representation of a real place – like Marlborough, New Zealand, Napa Valley, California, or Hunter Valley, Australia. Sometimes, a market flyer or shelf tag declares the wine to be a special purchase or an award winner at a local fair, too small for real competitors to bother with. At the astonishing price of U.S.$8.99 or less, the investment is so low there is little perceived risk.

This wine marketing ploy is rigged. It has all the elements of a carnival scam, including confusing messages, misdirection, and a low-risk, something-for-almost-nothing offer. The consumer, or "mark" as the carnies call them, ponies up the money, indulges a fantasy of being a supremely talented shopper who has made a great discovery and proudly carts a few bottles home. Unless it is going to be used for cooking, spiking punch, or cleaning auto parts, there is a good chance that some of it will bypass a human mouth, languish in a glass or spoil in an unfinished bottle, thereby completing an epic journey from a scoundrel's surplus tank to the kitchen drain.

"Abracadabra! . . . FINE WINE! Trust me!"

And so ends a tragic, eco-unfriendly saga of how some fermented grape juice traveled from a vineyard on one side of the world to a sewage system on the other. Truth be told, it would have been better if the birds had gotten the grapes.

On occasion, a consumer will self-validate his or her shopping prowess by declaring the wine to be excellent and telling others about the discovery. Psychologists have a term for this: Dissonance Reduction. Simply stated, no one wants to feel they were fooled into making a bad purchase. So, to avoid feelings of regret, the buyer convinces himself that it was a good purchase and reinforces this belief by recommending it to others. Admit it: Haven't you been misled on occasion by the recommendations of others – including professional reviewers who were more persuaded by a wine's pedigree than its quality?

Despite that sour note, there is economic benefit. Even in that tiny transaction, a little money is made by a herd of people, each punching the ticket as it passes their stall: Manufacturers of mechanical harvesting equipment, producers of chemical sprays, suppliers of stainless steel tanks and pumps, glass blowers, label printers, cardboard-box builders, truckers, ocean transporters, customs authorities, logistics firms, multiple taxing agencies, fuel refiners, wine importers, wine distributors, retailers, and an army of lawyers and accountants supporting them all – everyone taking a share of a price that has been known to go as low as U.S.$1.99 per 750ml bottle on some domestic wines. Who says making wine isn't profitable?

If you question for a moment who does and who does not make money from making wine, consider this simple example from New Zealand. One metric ton of New Zealand Sauvignon Blanc grapes from Marlborough will yield approximately 780 liters of finished wine. For the past decade, this wine has set the standard for a premium-priced, crisp, white, varietal in the U.K., U.S., and Australian markets. Yet despite its lofty position, and the accepted fact that Sauvignon Blanc is essentially "made" in the vineyard, those who "made" it only receive about NZ$1.50 per liter. The New Zealand government collects an additional NZ$2.61 in excise tax for every liter sold in country, plus 15% GST (Goods and Services Tax). The rest goes to bottle manufacturers, shippers, importers, distributors, and retailers.

Other profit-sucking scenarios can be found in the three-tier sales structure in the United States, where many states use their taxing and regulatory power to prohibit or restrict direct-to-consumer sales. This is accomplished by forcing sales to flow through their own licensed distributors and retailers and requiring, in some cases, expensive registration per label. Fundamentally, it's a protection racket for state distributors and retailers, severely constraining interstate commerce and short-changing the consumer by pushing up prices and restricting choice.

These are just two examples. Taxing authorities and protection of special interests are not just U.S. and New Zealand phenomena, and they are not the only challenge to small artisan wineries. The real profiteer behind the wine industry is the network of multi-national producers, distribution players, and trading parasites that squeeze the small producer and diminish market prospects.

To some extent, however, direct-to-consumer sales, electronic commerce, and greater emphasis on cellar-door/tasting-room sales has the potential to favorably alter archaic wine distribution models. The advent of internet-based wine sales, the geometric growth of social networks and word-of-mouth referrals, and the proliferation of small, independent wine clubs and retail networks are drawing more thoughtful consumers away from the "carnival barking" of the supermarket wine aisle.

It is important for the wine consumer to remember a fundamental principle of carnival economics – the illusion of choice. To separate marks from their money the carnival operator presents a lot of games and choices and the appearance of fair competition. But they really don't care where you play because all your money ends up in the same pocket.

If you doubt the validity of this comparison of carnivals with the wine industry, take a look at the brand portfolios of the top ten global wine producers. You will find that most of the choices you think you have in the wine section at the supermarket or the big discount chain store are really controlled by very few corporate "pockets."

The carnival never leaves town.

CHAPTER 6

Brand Burning in the Supermarkets

The world is awash with wine – enough to fill 140 million average-sized bath tubs each year. Producers are desperate to reduce inventories. Dumping product below cost is considered better than opening the tap and pouring it down the drain. At the prices offered by some brokers, large retail chains are now able to earn a decent margin on what would otherwise have been a loss leader. Unfortunately, these chains are doing something more devious. They are selling wine at or below cost simply to fill carts with groceries. Though loss-leading products are nothing new, undermining an entire product category serves nobody in the long term. As a friend of ours sarcastically stated, "They will burn a brand simply to heat water for morning tea."

Consider the recent and bloody skirmish over the Annie's Lane Clare Valley Shiraz range (750ml) between grocery outlets in Australia.

The Annie's Lane range had a recommended retail price (RRP) of AUD$20.99. In late August 2010, some Tasmanian independent grocers ran it at AUD$11.50. The next week, First Choice, a supermarket chain, ran a national campaign at AUD$8.99. Dan Murphy's, a liquor supermarket chain, then entered the fray, lowering the price to AUD$7.90. Two days later, First Choice ran a huge national campaign at AUD$7.50, and then Dan Murphy's offered it on radio for AUD$6.60. After ten days of advertising trench warfare, the price had plummeted to 69% off the RRP and 43% off the original discounted price, meaning the wine was selling well below wholesale.

"They will burn a brand simply to heat water for morning tea."

What effect did this have on the Annie's Lane brand? It cheapened it, and made it harder to sell at the RRP or indeed any price above AUD$6.60, making it an unattractive loser for any chain in the future. This is an example of how a brand can be "burned," after which retailers relegate it to a permanent bargain bin or refuse to stock it all. It also reinforces a perception that the wine was over-priced at the start and is better suited to binge drinking than a nice dinner with friends at home.

Fire Sale

Were this an isolated example it might not be cause for concern, but there have been similar cases all over the world. The consumer reaction is obvious – it is a wine-buying bonanza.

But what does this mean for the viability of the wine industry? While celebrating all the great bargains, we might want to consider the potential long-term consequences of this trend:

- **Industry restructuring.** As margins evaporate, industrial producers are forced to realign portfolios. Assets are dumped to clean up balance sheets. Cost reduction is paramount. Investment in product quality, research, and innovation are distant considerations.

- **Industry consolidation.** Large producers acquire smaller wineries lacking the scale to compete on price. They may maintain the brand to retain acquired customers, until the cost-driven decline in quality drives them away.

- **Reduction of consumer choice.** While the number of brands available may remain static or even increase as new labels are tested, management of those brands is concentrated with fewer producers. The control over distribution by monolithic producers squeezes others off the shelf.

- **Social responsibility.** Alcohol abuse is becoming a central concern for wine industry associations, as wine has the dubious distinction of being more potent per unit of volume than either beer or ready-to-drink beverages.

- **Polarizing the product category.** The stampede toward sub-$20 wine means fewer wines are available in the higher-quality, middle-price categories. The era of diverse selection in the still accessible $50–$70 bottle range may be coming to an end.

- **Destruction of an endangered species – the small artisan producer.** Many small artisan winemakers already are being forced to shut down. Access to the remaining unique and delightful artisan choices is all but disappearing from the retail landscape. Industry diversity is being replaced by the homogeneity of oligopoly.

The above list brings to mind a boa constrictor – or more specifically its victim. A boa constrictor kills by wrapping a few coils around its prey. Every time the prey exhales, the snake grips more tightly, until the victim suffocates. The prey is an active participant in its own death. This is not so unlike artisan winemakers who become unwitting accomplices in their own demise by giving in to the industry trends mentioned above. Every attempt they make to adapt to this environment is like "exhaling," which then allows the big producers to further restrict the artisan wine-maker's choices.

As the prices are squeezed at retail levels, each entity in the supply chain (including the taxing authorities) correspondingly squeezes the others to protect margins. It's a domino effect that trickles all the way down to the vineyard, with devastating effects. Each year more wineries respond to this squeeze by either cutting costs, loading more fruit on the vine, or both to hopefully increase revenue. Unfortunately, this con-tributes to a glut of lower-quality wine from grapes grown under sub-optimal conditions. As the supply of low-quality wine increases, the producers' price per liter drops further and it becomes even more diffi-cult for smaller wineries to survive.

The solution to this suffocation has been within reach for a long time. However, it seems to have evaded many of the emerging wine-produc-ing countries. The French appellation system, Appelation d'Origine Con-trôlée (AOC), which restricts yield, creates quality standards, and taxes or penalizes brand-damaging practices, may serve as a useful model for the global wine industry.[1]

For those whose independent spirit won't be bound by rigid grape grow-ing and winemaking rules, less restrictive standards that still support minimum levels of authenticity and quality can be developed. One such example – Waiheke Island's Certified Wine program in New Zealand – applies a basic set of standards to stop such practices as brand free-loading (misrepresenting the region where the grapes were grown) which takes advantage of lax label laws and the absence of any mean-ingful regulatory enforcement. There is more detailed discussion of this program in Chapter 16.

One would think that minimum standards for any wine would be:

1. The contents of the bottle match what the label says.

2. The practices used to grow grapes and make the wine are environmentally sensitive.

3. The wine is free from standard faults that would prevent most government agencies from allowing it to be sold to the pub-lic.

And yet, even in regions of the world not governed by the often contentiously administered AOC, there is considerable resistance to even these basic standards.

This is probably one of the most obvious areas where strong-willed and independently minded artisans are their own worst enemy. Rather than oppose all bureaucracy on principle, they would be better served by championing a program that would prevent freeloaders from profiting off their regional brands without meeting minimum labeling, environmental, and quality-control standards. Unfortunately, trying to organize artisan producers is a real challenge. It is like trying to herd cats, and cats spend more time clawing at each other than cooperating with each other.

Reducing intrusions into a product category (e.g., an acclaimed wine region) from low-quality and low-cost substitutes reduces price undercutting by those who do not meet minimum standards. Absent some level of regional control, there is little that the small artisan producers can do to protect their brands and businesses from being destroyed by large businesses capable of squeezing margins to a level that can only be sustained by high-volume, low-cost, low-quality operations.

While the daily brand burning in the supermarket aisles may appear to be a consumer bonanza, it is in reality another variation of the oldest sales trick in the book – bait and switch. Lure consumers to the supermarket under the pretense of picking up fine wine at a bargain price and instead supply a low-cost, low-quality substitute that has even higher margin potential for the producer. Once the higher-cost and higher-quality artisans are burned out or choked to death, nothing stands in the way of the Grape-a-hol manufacturers' unfettered access to consumers' wallets.

CHAPTER 7

The False Economy of Cheap Wine

When is a bargain not a bargain? Maybe when you're paying a 450% premium for an alcoholic beverage made from fermented grape juice? Follow the math.

In New Zealand, a producer of Sauvignon Blanc will earn approximately NZ$1.50 at today's price for the grapes needed to make one bottle of wine.[1] Add to that the cost of mass-production winemaking and bottling and you are up to around NZ$2.00 a bottle, give or take a few cents. Let's assume the producer is making zero profit (breaking even is an optimistic scenario for many artisan producers). Add to this the government excise tax of NZ$2.03 per bottle and transportation costs of about NZ$0.50 per bottle and you are up to NZ$4.53 per bottle. Now add the distributor margin of 30% (some are a bit more and some a bit less), a retailer margin of 30% (again some are more and some are less), and 15% GST (Goods and Services Tax) and voila! Two dollars' worth of wine is now NZ$10.50 per bottle. Since most are discounting even further, you will most likely see that NZ$10.50 wine selling for NZ$8.99 or less, meaning that several people in the chain (except the government) are cutting their margins even further.

Two Questions:

1. Putting aside the obvious fact that these are "dumping" prices and are not sustainable, how much care, passion, and craftsmanship do you really think these producers can put into that wine knowing they are being paid less than it costs to grow and ferment the grapes?

2. A more baffling question is why people believe they are getting a bargain when paying NZ$8.99 for less than NZ$2.00 worth of that same beverage? That represents a 450% mark up. Still feel good about the NZ$0.40 worth of wine staring back at you in that one glass that cost you NZ$1.80 or more?

If you think this is only a problem in New Zealand, check out Australia's 29% WET (Wine Equalization Tax) or other trade-barrier taxing policies in other parts of the world. If you have any doubt, the real way to make money in the wine business is to be the government. In New Zealand, the government collects NZ$3.19 (NZ$2.03 in excise and NZ$1.17 in GST) or a whopping 35% for that NZ$8.99 bottle of Sauvignon Blanc sold in the supermarket. In other words, for every bottle's worth of grapes a New Zealand grower produces, the government rakes in more than one and half times the grower's revenue.

" . . . and unfortunately we have to pay SOMETHING for the actual wine."

The impact of this lopsided arrangement introduces a kind of Gresham's Law to the wine industry. Gresham's Law is an economic principle stating that bad money (e.g., paper currency not pegged to a valuable commodity like gold and therefore artificially valued) drives out good money (e.g., currency based on a gold standard) when governments mandate that both currencies be accepted as equal in value. This happens because consumers will prefer to use the "bad money" in transactions rather than the "good money," keeping the good currency for themselves and thereby creating a shortage of it and forcing the government to put more bad currency in circulation. In the wine industry multiple factors are conspiring to produce a similar phenomenon, with the ever increasing amounts of Grape-a-hol in circulation crowding out fine artisan wines.

The producers best equipped to make profits with cheap-wine economics are the very big ones who can drive the cost of production down through economies of scale.

Rising transport, material, and labor costs, tax increases, scarce and expensive working-capital financing, and price pressure from retailers reverberates down the value chain to producers. Unable to absorb additional costs and price pressure, some artisan wineries have already abandoned product improvement and taste distinction. Instead, they are resorting to cost-cutting, yield-enhancement practices and bulk sales that add to wine surpluses, reduce wine quality, increase the pool of cheap Grape-a-hol, and reinforce low prices. This wine industry form of Gresham's Law is a financial volcano. When it erupts, the economic heat and pressure will push out enough lava to bury many small wineries.

Perhaps now it is clear why so many small artisan producers depend on selling direct to their customers by offering loyalty clubs through their cellar door or over the internet. Not wishing to compete with their retailers, they will generally only offer a discounted price if the consumer commits to regular purchases in advance. Even with the shipping and handling, it works out better for both the producer and the customer. And don't worry about the government – it still gets the lion's share of the proceeds.

If you think these numbers are different for more expensive wine, think again. Even a wine retailing for NZ$100 a bottle returns less than 35% of that to the grape grower and winemaker for their efforts. However, it is worth considering how much more passion and craftsmanship can be invested in a wine that is worth about NZ$7 a glass than one worth NZ$0.40 a glass. A little long division shows that an expensive wine may cost ten times more than the one on the discount shelf, but the value in the bottle is likely to be almost 20 times greater.

Despite higher prices, artisan fine wines represent good value because most producers spend more on product quality than they recover from sales. The extra time and effort these craftspeople invest in making their wine is seldom reflected in their cost calculations. They either lose track of, or completely ignore, the true costs of growing grapes and making wine. Few place economic value on their personal time or the cost-of-capital associated with family assets that are essentially loaned for free to their business. If an artisan producer paid someone else to do what they often do for free, and paid interest on capital to purchase all the assets they own to make wine, their cost of goods sold would likely double.

As one artisan winemaker friend said, "I would be delighted to sell my wine for what it cost me to make it, but I don't think my customers could stomach the huge increase in price."

If you want the cheapest price per unit of volume, go for the Grape-a-hol. If you want the best value for money, artisan wines are hard to top.

Does it really take 200 years, as the Baron Rothschild suggested, to turn a profit in the fine wine business? If not, who is making profit in the current sales environment? Sadly it is not those making some of the best wines but rather those selling Grape-a-hol into the mass market. The producers best equipped to succeed (make profits) with cheap-wine economics are the very big ones who can drive the cost of production down through economies of scale. Is that really the future of the wine industry – minimally palatable alcoholic beverages made from fermented grape juice, with most brands controlled by a cost-fixated oligopoly?

Absent shifts in taxation and regulatory policy, the artisan winemaker's survival is in jeopardy. Apparently many of the government agencies who treat small artisan producers with the same callous insensitivity they treat resilient staff of large corporate producers have never heard the fable about the farmer's plow horse.

With the cost of feed rising, a farmer realized that he could occasionally skip a meal for his plow horse without any decline in the horse's productivity. After a few weeks he started skipping a meal every other day. Still the horse kept on working and the farmer was saving a lot of money on feed, so he decided to skip a few more meals. Finally, just when he managed to get the poor horse down to only one feeding a week, it up and died on him.

The regulatory and taxation policies for many wine-producing countries are contributing to a similar fate for many small artisan producers. The combination of falling consumer prices and sustained levels of excise tax revenue have placed the industry at a precarious tipping point. Collapse is on the horizon for the artisan wine segment if regulatory and taxing authorities don't come to their senses.

CHAPTER 8

Day Traders, Dilettantes, Parasites, and Pilot Fish

The following is a reconstruction of an actual conversation that took place between one of our staff and a caller not so long ago.

"Good morning, Destiny Bay Wine Imports."
"Hi. Who is this? Who does the hiring?"
"We have no positions open at this time."
"You don't have a distributor in North Carolina. Do you? I'm your guy."
"Are you a licensed distributor? What is the name of your company?"
"Well, I'm between jobs. But, I know wine. I used to work in a liquor store. Here's the deal. You don't have to pay me. Just send me the wine. I'll make the rounds of the restaurants and collect orders. You just cover my expenses and a 20% commission. I'll work under your license."
"Is this a joke?"
"No joke. I know it sounds too good to be true. But, everyone says I've got a great palate. I know all the sommeliers in the state and I love your Sauvignon Blanc. I drink it all the time. I can really get behind it."
"We don't produce Sauvignon Blanc wines. We produce Bordeaux-style, Cabernet blends."
"Oh, I must have gotten you confused with that other bay."
"We appreciate your interest. But, we are not hiring at this time."
"OK. Cabernet, huh? Are you interested in buying genuine Napa Valley Cabernet? Only two bucks a gallon."
"I thought you were between jobs."
"I know people. I'll make the introduction and you can pay me a finder's fee."
"Sorry. We only sell our own wine. Thanks again for your interest. This has been very entertaining. Good day."

There are a lot of interesting and impressive people in the wine business. There also are a fair share of sycophants, snobs, fools, and frauds. Like many industries characterized by fanciful notions of celebrity, artistry, social gatherings, good cheer, or dreams of life in pastoral settings, the wine business, and particularly vineyards and wineries, are a magnet for the best and the worst of wine society. Unfortunately, shysters like the fellow who wanted to sell us "genuine" Napa Valley Cabernet for U.S.$2 a gallon dominate the industry's cast of characters.

When we first began importing wine into the U.S., we attended a wine tasting event. At this event another attendee came up and started a conversation, which we've reconstructed below.

> "Hi, Mark (we all had name badges on), I'm John. I overheard that you are importing a high-end wine from New Zealand. Very cool. I import Italian dessert wines. Great stuff. I was wondering if you were able to make importing and distribution a full-time job. I started this part time after a trip to Italy. But, I can't sell enough wine to make this full time. I need a day job to make a living. I thought it would be easy. But, no one wants to give an unknown Italian winery and an unknown distributor a chance. Instead of a business, it's more like a part-time hobby going nowhere. I feel like one of those small-fry day traders dabbling in stock trading to avoid looking for a real job. Wishful thinking. What do you think I should do?"
> "I think you should tell the winery the truth."
> "What do you mean?"
> "Do you have an import license? A distribution license?"
> "No licenses. I plan to apply when the business takes off."
> "How did you bring the wine into the U.S.?"
> "A broker did it for me. Just enough to taste with some sommeliers and wine shops. If I get orders, I'll arrange shipping."
> "How did you convince the winery to let you represent them?"
> "All of the U.S. distributors they contacted were unwilling to take on a new winery, especially a small unknown winery with no marketing program in the U.S."
> "So, you have no licenses. No customers. No experience. No operating capital. No prospects. Does that sum it up?"
> "Well, yes. But, once I have some orders all that will change. So, what do you think?"
> "If it were me, I'd tell the winery the truth. To you, this is a harmless gamble – a chance to put your toe in the water. To them, it's a serious business with serious investment behind it . . . as well as their lives and probably a lot of debt. Regardless of the purity of your intentions, you're stringing them along."

We never did follow up and to this day we feel we should have been even more honest with the guy about how he wasn't helping his Italian "client" and how he was probably tainting perceptions of their brand and their wine. The kindest characterization of this fellow is that he was a dilettante without a clue.

The wine business, and particularly vineyards and wineries, are a magnet for the best and the worst of wine society.

This is not an isolated example. It's just another variation on what happens when small artisan producers come up against a parochial and insulated distribution network that views artisans as low-volume nuisances. Out of desperation, the artisan wineries fall prey to pretenders, charlatans, and scammers. These are the wine industry parasites, the equivalent of the proverbial used car salesman, the weekend real estate broker, and the day traders who believe they can trade securities better than the pros.

The parasites are a surprisingly heterogeneous bunch that live in the supply chain and feed off each other and the consumer. They include parasitic producers who leverage a region, varietal, or style to sell poor specimens at the highest possible price to unsuspecting trades people and their end customers. Like leeches, they bleed and weaken the industry.

"Okay, which one of you clowns tried to sell 10,000 bottles of Chateau 'La Feet' to the Catholic church as communion wine?"

Parasitic behavior in the sense of exploitation is also evident in the actions of many taxing authorities that siphon cash out of an industry without regard for the wider economic and social consequences.

Government short-sightedness is not limited to taxation policy. It frequently includes trade protectionism. The most notable example is the three-tier laws in many U.S. states, which have already been touched on in Chapters 1 and 5. To protect distributors and retailers within their borders, some states disallow direct sales to consumers by out-of-state wineries, requiring that all wine sales go through their own state-licensed distributors and retailers. Despite the questions this raises regarding interstate commerce laws and the free flow of goods across state borders, legislators in these states are perpetually lobbied by local distribution and retail trade associations to keep these protectionist laws in place. The result is that these special interest groups have license to take another bite out of wine-producer margins. The result is a margin squeeze that ultimately takes its toll on product quality and the high-value-added, low-profit segment of the market, which is generally dominated by artisan producers.

Many large supermarket chains are particularly diabolical examples of parasitic behavior. They often use wine as a loss leader to lure customers to their stores. Food margins tend to be miniscule. To make a profit, they need volume. As noted earlier, reducing wine prices to below the cost of production levels attracts customers and generates grocery pull-through volume. Unfortunately, when the national and regional supermarket chains and franchises negotiate for lower prices to support this strategy, everyone on the supply chain is squeezed. Moreover, as discussed in Chapter 6, price wars can burn brands in the marketplace, relegating a wine to permanently low status among consumers. Even the large Grape-a-hol producers are victims of this practice and feel powerless to stand up to the major supermarket chains that simply threaten to drop one supplier's portfolio in favor of another.

As noted in the Preface, in 2010 the Stonebridge Research Group reported there were roughly a quarter million wines for sale in the United States and that in the first half of 2011 the U.S. Treasury & Tax Bureau issued no fewer than 70,000 new certificates of label approval. By October of 2011, they were operating with a backlog of double that number.

Stonebridge Research Group also noted that over the past two decades the number of U.S. distributors has declined by 90%, to around 700. That means 250,000 wines are being represented by only 700 distributors to 50,000 retail stores and nearly 300,000 restaurants, hotels, and other on-premises sales outlets. The climate is cutthroat and in recent years nearly every distributor has reduced slow-moving inventory and eliminated brands of small producers that cannot afford aggressive marketing, ad buying, and promotional discounting. The proliferation of brands has meant that the surviving distributors have been forced to rationalize their portfolios in order to protect their own margins, stay in business, and avoid forced consolidation.

This distribution environment is not just a U.S. phenomenon. It is a global problem that forces small artisan wineries to pursue marginal distribution partners and accept terms of trade that promise much and deliver little. It is no wonder so many artisans avoid distribution outside their immediate geographic location, thereby denying a larger community access to many of our industry's inspired products.

And finally there are the pilot fish. In Nature, pilot fish have a symbiotic relationship with sharks, feeding on the parasites that threaten the health of sharks. The relationship benefits both parties and is not unlike the relationship between some wine writers and producers of Grape-a-hol – or, more recently, large-volume private-label wines essentially manufactured by large supermarket chains in order to capture more of the product margin. In writing about mass-produced factory wines as though they reflect the same craftsmanship and provenance of small, regional artisan winemakers, these quasi-independent writers promote a false equivalency between Grape-a-hol and artisan winemaking. The benefit to the writer is a stable source of work and income. The benefit to the factory producer is endorsed membership in the "fine wine" product category. They help each other but diminish the broader product category and drive the wine industry further down the food chain among commoditized alcoholic beverages.

Artisan wine producers on the other hand spend most of their resources on the single-minded pursuit of their craft. Very little resource is left to generate the commercial visibility necessary to attract consumers and build a fan base. If they swim in the same place with the sharks and pilot fish they are easily picked off or turned into bait.

Ironically, however, the same profession that helps large producers undermine the wine industry also possesses the power to celebrate and promote the diversity, distinctiveness, and expressiveness that is the hallmark of artisan winemaking. There are many committed and passionate writers who visit the wineries, observe the practices, and delve into the skills and aspirations of those who grow the grapes and craft the wines. These writers bring context and texture to the appreciation of these wines. They help us all understand the importance of terroir and the personal struggle that is behind carefully crafted fine artisan wines.

The reality is that without wine writers, the smaller, craft-focused members of the industry would have little protection against the predators and little chance of survival. In reality we do not need fewer writers, just more of them focused on telling the personal stories of thousands of inspired artisans which, without the help of these storytellers, would be lost to all of us.

Absent the contribution from skilled wine storytellers, the industry would be shaped by corporate producers with well-funded marketing programs. The wine business would quickly devolve into a homogeneous market of Grape-a-hol varietals. Terroir and character would be papered over with advertisements and carnival barkers would be competing for the consumer dollar with promotional deals and theatrical hyperbole – all of it would be content-free noise.

CHAPTER 9

The Hubris of Wine Writing:
The Good, the Bad, and the Ugly

There is no formal certification, registration, licensing, or training program to become a wine writer - you simply just declare yourself to be one.

Helping consumers sift through the bargain bin at the end of the supermarket aisle might be a good gig for some writers, but it is really a terrible waste of knowledge, training, and talent.

Make no mistake, there are some truly talented and experienced people out there who have earned and command respect, and they can make or break a producer - large or small - with the stroke of a pen. Even those with lesser reputations wield considerable influence in an industry where factory and artisan wine producers try to occupy the same space in a consumer's mind and compete for the visibility that media gatekeepers can offer. Ratings, stars, and colorful metaphors are their stock-in-trade, and confused consumers rely on their guidance to weave their way through a dizzying array of varietals, regions, and labels.

But who rates the critics? How does a consumer know whom to trust? How does the consumer separate the ethical, skilled, and trained critic from those pretending to know what they are doing? Certainly this must be of concern to those writers who are studious, skilled, and dedicated to their work. Are the many pretenders diluting the influence of the truly informed reviewers? Are the dilettantes giving really good critics a bad name by cheapening the endeavor with hollow opinions and content-free text?

A very important issue for wine writers, critics, and judges revolves around independence of opinion and conflict of interest. In New Zealand, a new group of wine writers was formed specifically to address issues surrounding pay for reviews. Calling themselves the Wine Writers of New Zealand, 25 of the country's leading wine writers have signed a pledge that both recognizes the problem and makes an explicit statement of their code of practice. Following is an excerpt from their "declaration of independence" included on their website:

> It would not be acceptable to the public for critics in other fields to be paid by those whom they are reviewing. We believe that the public and wine producers are entitled to expect that an equally high standard of independence and integrity is applied to the field of wine reviewing.
>
> Direct payments from wine producers to writers for published reviews remove the independence that is crucial to a critic's integrity, and upon which their reputation rests. They also create a potential for bias, whether actual or perceived.
>
> We are committed to the interests of the public and to protecting the reputation for integrity of wine writers in New Zealand. As such, we will not accept any direct payments from wine producers for published reviews.[1]

While we agree with the spirit of this declaration, striving for true independence (e.g., being completely free from the influence, guidance, or control of another or others) may be a standard too ambitious to achieve and impractical for those who earn their livelihood reviewing and judging wines. As former business consulting partners in one of the largest accounting and audit firms in the world, we are all too familiar with the limits and frustrations of rigid rules. However, avoiding conflicts of interest, and disclosing those conflicts when they exist, is certainly attainable.

We understand and accept that writers and critics must earn a living. The time and effort it takes to review and comment on wines carries a cost that must be born by someone. Clearly, when a winemaker agrees to pay for a review in advance, the critic is placed in an awkward and untenable position. Nobody is going to pay for a bad review and reviewers know that. So, is there any place for paid wine reviews in this business? We think there is, as long as there is full disclosure of the facts. Celebrity endorsements are valuable marketing tools and when a critic is paid for a review they are in fact endorsing a product. There is nothing inherently wrong with this so long as the consumer is not misled into believing it is an independent evaluation. In our view, the sin is not in the act of accepting pay for reviews, but in covering up the fact that it happened. Perhaps reviews that are the result of this process need to contain a statement similar to that which is included at the bottom of political advertisements: "Paid for by . . . "

Whether a critic chooses to accept money, favors, special treatment, or other inducements for reviews is a personal decision. And, as long as any conflicts of interest are disclosed to the public, then no harm is done. After all, it is up to the individual to decide which products he or she will "endorse," but if their review is positioned as independent or the consumer is led to believe by act of omission that it is independent, then that is a deceptive practice which should be discouraged.

Another issue when considering wine writers is determining what is important. Where does the skill lie – in the judging or the writing? Research has consistently demonstrated that wine experts are no better than an average person in identifying quality. In one meta-analysis titled "Empirical Foundations of Wine Expertise," which was published in the *Australian & New Zealand Grapegrower & Winemaker* in 2006, Angus Hughson notes:

> Another activity that experts regularly perform is to assess the quality of wine samples. The results of such analyses are important for the wine consumer as buying and cellaring decisions are often based on the opinion of experts. So far, three studies have evaluated the agreement among experts and novices as to what constitutes a high-quality wine. In each of the studies (Young, 1986, 1995; Solomon, 1988) the results show that there is little consensus among both experts and novices as to which wine is best among a set of samples. In fact, in regard to perceived quality, there is more agreement among novices than experts. Thus, there is as yet no evidence to show that wine experts, and perhaps even sensory experts as a whole (Roberts and Vickers, 1994), are more competent than novices in the assessment of quality.[2]

From 2005 to 2008 Robert Hodgson conducted a three-year study of judge reliability at the California State Fair in Sacramento, which hosts the oldest commercial wine competition in North America and only accepts wine industry professionals as judges.[3] Though prior studies had already demonstrated a lack of agreement between judges, Hodgson's examined individual judge consistency, as measured by a judge's ability to consistently evaluate samples of the same wine multiple times in a blind tasting.

Hodgson found that only 10% of the judges were able to consistently give the same or a very similar rating to samples of the same wine tasted multiple times. Moreover, 10% of judges gave the same samples notably different ratings, ranging from gold-medal quality to no-medal quality in successive tasting sessions. The other 80% also produced varied, but less dramatically different, judgments.

Similarly, Roman Weil found in two studies that even tasters who could distinguish between excellent and appalling vintages didn't agree on which was which.[4] You begin to wonder whether wine writers, expert or not, are even necessary. Maybe, as one colleague insists, they just have a better vocabulary.

No wonder the top two criteria applied by consumers in selecting a wine are prior experience in tasting the wine and a recommendation from a friend or someone working in the store.[5] With personal networks and recommendations becoming paramount, perhaps the greatest value offered by the wine writer is the provision of education, perspective, and opinion on wine and its socio-cultural and geographical context.

The data are compelling – and more than a little dispiriting. Many wine writers are dedicated, studious, conscientious, and have well-trained palates. Yet, one often wonders if these palates are being worn out – used up as it were – on wines that are more effectively sold on price and label appearance rather than the intrinsic characteristics of what is contained in the bottle.

Seeking third-party advice is generally advisable when making acquisitions of considerable cost with potential risk. How much risk is there really in purchasing a bottle of wine that may even cost as much as US$30? Unless it reeks of sulfur, wet cardboard, dead mice, moldy dirt, Band-Aids, vinegar, or other noxious odors, or tastes equally foul, is there really a benefit to knowing what somebody else thinks it tastes like?

The good wine writers evaluate more than technical merit. The really gifted ones talk about artistic expression – how the style, construction, and character of a wine reflects its origin. Is it a typical example of a style, variety, or region? Are there important nuances and subtleties to the wine that might help an interested customer expand their own wine knowledge? In one year most good wine writers have opportunities to taste more wine from more regions – often at the source – than the rest of us do in a lifetime. They can offer perspectives and insights that enhance the customer's experience with wine. Relegating that talent – and occasionally genius – to commenting on factory-produced standard product seems a horrible misuse of their skills and, according to the research, is an unreliable and often meaningless activity.

Our view is that wine writers and critics should help the rest of us navigate through the maze of information about regional, varietal, and style differences so that we can make informed choices and avoid disappointment when we decide to purchase something special.

**"Hmm ... essence of factory lint with overtones of insect dander
and a hint of machine oil."**

Helping consumers sift through the bargain bin at the end of the supermarket aisle might be a good gig for some writers, but it is really a terrible waste of knowledge, training, and talent.

CHAPTER 10

Wine Competitions and the Gambler's Fallacy

Y ou can't win the lottery if you don't buy a ticket. A fellow wine-maker once told us why he entered competitions: "It is pretty much a lottery. You pay your money, send your wine in and if you win an award, great. If not, you just move on to the next one. Unless your wine is truly awful you will win a gold medal eventually." This is a classic example of the Gambler's Fallacy, the belief that a random event is more or less likely to occur because it has or has not happened recently. This flawed reasoning helps guarantee profits for casinos.

Wait a second. The sharp-eyed reader will have caught the word "random" in the previous paragraph. Are we implying that the outcome of wine competitions is random? Is our winemaker friend suffering under a delusion that his winning card will show up eventually, if he keeps trying?

In a word, yes.

Whatever your point of view, whether you are a promoter, participant, or spectator, wine competitions will influence your perception of the wines. Your perception will also be influenced whether you have won or lost or have been pleased or disappointed after tasting the top-rated wines. There is, however, an interesting perceptual paradox for winemakers who participate in these events.

Many winemakers will privately express the view that wine competitions are among the biggest hoaxes ever perpetrated on the wine-consuming public. However, these same winemakers believe that they are indispensable hoaxes. After all, competitions offer visibility, a chance at a medal, and a potential increase in sales. Further, in some of the lesser contests, they can expect weaker competition and less-qualified judges. Most consumers will not know the difference between a gold medal from a major competition and one from a minor one anyway. So, is this a rational market strategy for an artisan winery searching for recognition, or is it a classic example of the Gambler's Fallacy?

"**And the winner is . . .**"

The Wine Institute of California lists 31 major annual competitions in North America on its website. There are hundreds more in county fairs and locally sponsored events. In a bid for visibility in the midst of the thousands of wine labels sold in North America each year, wineries annually spend millions of dollars in entry fees, shipping, and travel to participate in at least a few of these events. They are gambling on a significant return on investment from a win. After all, awards are consumer signposts and do sell wine – or do they?

In an article titled "How American Consumers Select Wine" published in *Wine Business Monthly* in June 2008, Liz Thach described the results of a global wine marketing study executed by ten collaborating universities.[1] The top two reasons for selecting a wine in a retail store were prior experience in tasting the wine and a recommendation from a friend or someone working in the store (as noted in Chapter 9). The third factor was varietals, then origin and brand. Having won a medal had significantly less sway than the other reasons and only scored higher in influence than having read about the wine, suggesting that consumers were not especially influenced by medals when purchasing wine in retail stores.

Robert Hodgson's 2009 article in the *Journal of Wine Economics,* "An Analysis of the Concordance among 13 U.S. Wine Competitions," also provides some interesting insights.[2] His examination of the results of 13 U.S. wine competitions found that "(1) there is almost no consensus among the 13 wine competitions regarding wine quality, (2) for wines receiving a Gold medal in one or more competitions, it is very likely that the same wine received no award at another, (3) the likelihood of receiving a Gold medal can be statistically explained by chance alone." This led him to conclude that "perhaps consumers are beginning to realize . . . that winning gold medals may be more a matter of chance than a predictor of quality."

If you are like us, you have probably tried a number of disappointing gold and silver medal wines. We've learned our lesson. Medals can be deceptive.

In August of 2010, the New York Cork Report blog provided a thoughtful and well-reasoned explanation for why they would no longer be participating as judges in wine competitions.[3] The key points of their rationale follow:

- Medals only confuse consumers instead of educating them.

- The very act of blind judging a wide range of wines should be viewed as a parlor game and not some official declaration of merit.

- Blind judging robs the evaluators of the most significant parts of the wine - its context. Medals are awarded in a fashion that almost appears to be random. "There is ample evidence that judging is like throwing darts."

- Judging in mass competitions is putting wine into just about the least most suitable place for good evaluation and enjoyment.

The editors conclude that "consumers don't know which wineries entered a particular competition and which didn't, they don't know the judges and what the judges are looking for, they don't know how many medals were awarded, and they don't know what a medal is supposed to signify." They close by asking industry colleagues to join them in declining invitations to judge these events.

Frankly, we agree with the New York Cork Report and would add one other major problem to their list – the carry-over and order effect. This is a common problem (see Ronald S. Jackson, *Wine Tasting: A Professional Handbook*, 2009) that occurs when wines are tasted in sequence, as they often are in wine competitions. Simply stated, the order in which wines are tasted has a profound impact on how they are experienced. You can test this for yourself with a range of wines or perform an even simpler experiment with your own palate. Taste a wine and make some mental notes about what you are experiencing. Then take a sip of orange juice or very strong coffee, swirl it around in your mouth and swallow. Now taste the wine again. Unless you have severe sensory impairment, the second sip of the wine will not taste like the first sip. This phenomenon is well known to wine judges and critics, and to be fair, they generally try to avoid the problem by cleansing their palate between sips, taking breaks, or eating something neutral during the tasting process.

The best control is time. Most skilled critics will taste a wine repeatedly over a reasonable period of time, and occasionally come back to it later to confirm their perception. Naturally such a protocol is not conducive to large competitions with hundreds, if not thousands, of entries that must be tasted in a compressed timeframe. Imagine tasting a hundred highly acidic Sauvignon Blancs over a few hours. By the end of the day you would probably feel like you needed a palate transplant.

This is the reality of wine competitions, or "sip and spit contests," as some call them. However, absent an industry epiphany, event promoters will continue to organize competitions for profit and winemakers will continue to rely on them for visibility. And, of course, some consumers will continue to gravitate to medals for emotional reasons, while most store keepers will continue to rely on medals for business reasons.

Another problem with wine competitions relates to consumer psychology. A cursory review of research in this area reveals that as the number of product choices increases, consumers become more confused, more anxious, and less likely to purchase anything or try something new. By posting signs for medal winners, the supermarket or wine shop narrows the range of choices, reduces consumer anxiety, and facilitates a purchase in the absence of more powerful decision criteria. However, the lack of transparency regarding what other wines entered the competition, the circumstances of the judging, who the judges were, how many wines they tasted, and so on precludes a truly informed consumer decision and often showcases wines destined to disappoint the consumer.

If you are comparing one Grape-a-hol manufacturer with another, there will be a winner, but that winner is still Grape-a-hol. When award winners disappoint consumers, we submit this diminishes trust in medals and undermines the industry by failing to build an informed and trusting consumer base.

If you are like us, you have probably tried a number of disappointing gold and silver medal wines, chosen, perhaps, because they were "value-priced." We've learned our lesson. Medals can be deceptive.

What are consumers to do? What can producers do to inform customers rather than engage in an elaborate deception that ultimately diminishes product loyalty?

Not long ago we asked a well-known New Zealand wine critic why he invested time writing reviews about low-cost, mass-produced wines when his own interests and talents made him particularly well suited to critiquing more nuanced wines. His first reaction to our question was surprise, followed by silence while he considered an answer – which never came. But, of course, the question was general and posed in a rhetorical fashion so the discussion moved on. We suspect his hesitation was caused by ambivalence. On the one hand he felt the need to defend his actions and on the other he probably agreed with us.

Our argument was simple. Wine competitions could serve a more useful purpose by "grading" Grape-a-hol into quality levels like the "standard," "select," "choice," or "prime" designations are used for beef. That would provide consumers with more useful information on how to expend a limited food shopping budget. Let's face it, factory-produced Grape-a-hol is here to stay. If it is to become the primary wine choice, consumers should be offered better selection criteria.

A grading process based on standard quality designations would be hugely beneficial for consumers looking for choices based on price. Trying to tease out the quality difference between a bronze medal at the Decanter World Wine Awards and a gold medal from the Santa Clara County Fair is a decision few are prepared to face.

We believe experienced critics and Masters of Wine should focus their talents on helping the rest of us sort out the difference between wines produced by the dedicated rather than the deluded artisan winemakers. The distinctiveness and diversity of these non-factory wines beg for guidance from experienced palates that can encourage people to expand their tastes and cultivate interests in wines and styles that they otherwise might never consider.

It is clear, then, that there are many problems with large wine competitions, including transparency, reliability, carry-over and order effect, palate fatigue, personal bias, and time constraints. Yet, despite our criticism of this method of "scoring" wine, we believe that competitions could serve a useful purpose by helping consumers sift through quality variations in mass-produced wine. However, such a shift in thinking would require the world's producers of Grape-a-hol to admit that they are not in the fine wine product category and accept that sales of their product might actually be better served by a rating process that did not involve deception and creating confusion.

CHAPTER 11

Temperance, Tax, and Over-indulgence

Most artisan winemakers suffer from chronic doubt about their decision to focus on quality and distinctiveness as they struggle to cope with the economic consequences of that choice. This stress has been known to cause nightmares that unfold something like this:

> The phone rings. An eager voice on the other end says "Hello, are you the owner?"
>
> "Who's calling please?"
>
> "I represent a wine industry consultancy. We have been researching high-quality artisan wineries and believe we can dramatically increase your sales."
>
> "Thank you for your call, but we do not require assistance at this time."
>
> "Wait. Don't hang up. We attended the winery's open house and we went on the vineyard tour. We determined that there are some very obvious things you could be doing to drive up sales volume."
>
> "Would you like to share an example?"
>
> "Sure. I've got plenty of examples. You need to increase your yield per acre, so you can increase volume and reduce cost per unit. You're dropping too much fruit. I know you folks believe great wine starts in the vineyard and only the best grapes should make it to the winery. But, the economics don't work. Wine has become a volume business. Lower the cost, lower the price, and make profit on volume. Artistry is a quaint concept that will kill you economically. Save it for the brochure. It has no place in today's wine business. The artists are selling out or joining the conglomerates."
>
> "Well, that's an intriguing perspective but, I think we have a very competent vineyard and winery team and they place quality before volume and price, but thanks for calling."
>
> "Wait a minute. Let's talk marketing. You're marketing is all wrong and you are not taking advantage of the millennial buyers. That's where the volume is today. You have to sell lifestyle. Aspirational lifestyle. And you have to use social media. They buy lifestyle, they're price sensitive, and they buy whatever their Facebook friends are buying. Like Sheep."
>
> "I appreciate your call but I have work to do. Thank you and good bye."

Thankfully, few artisan winemakers actually receive calls like this and, if they did, even fewer would stay on the line long enough to hear the full pitch. Yet most are nevertheless haunted by the expensive choices they make in the name of quality. Should we drop less fruit? Does anybody really appreciate what we do? Do we have the right selling agent? Are we getting our message to the right people?

These doubts gnaw on the conscience of nearly all artisan winemakers. The nightmares of their Grape-a-hol cousins, on the other hand, tend to focus on not making return-on-investment targets.

Throughout this book we have been very critical of Grape-a-hol producers, primarily because we believe they are poaching the reputation of a craft refined by artisans all over the world for thousands of years.

If you visit any supermarket or chain liquor store and browse the boxed wine section you will find many of the products on display preposterously claiming to be "fine wine" while being priced at the equivalent of US$5.00 a bottle. This kind of marketing hyperbole reminds us of Joe Isuzu, a fictional spokesman in U.S. television advertisements for Isuzu automobiles and trucks in the late 1980s. Played by actor David Leisure, Joe Isuzu was a pathological liar who made outrageously exaggerated claims about Isuzu's cars, such as:

- "If I'm lying, may lightning hit my mother." ("Good luck, Mom!" flashes on screen.)
- "This car has more seats than the Houston Astrodome!"
- "Hi, I'm Joe Isuzu and I used my new Isuzu pickup truck to carry a 2,000lb cheeseburger."

The hypocrisy of such outrageous double-talk is not reserved solely for advertising claims. It also is evident among those who show concern for over-indulgence by young drinkers while fostering the conditions for producing and distributing ever cheaper Grape-a-hol.

Nowhere is the impact of cheap alcoholic beverage on behavior more noticeable than among young, price-sensitive drinkers. If the government and the wine lobby are really serious about curbing irresponsible drinking, they might first want to consider removing the substantial incentives to consume cheap wine and the pressures exerted on manufacturers to make their money by chasing the low-cost, high-volume profit model.

To prove this to yourself, all you need to do is visit the alcoholic beverage section of any supermarket or major liquor retail chain. Take a

"We're kicking off our 'Drink Responsibly' campaign with a 2 for 1 sale!"

calculator with you and check out the special deals on beer, wine, and ready-to-drink (RTD) beverages.

A quick scan of the current New Zealand beverage landscape would reveal the following:

- DB beer – two 15 packs of 330ml cans, 4% alcohol, for a total of NZ$40 (tax, license, and out the door). That works out to about NZ$1.25 per standard drink (12.7ml of alcohol by volume) and 320ml of carbonated water and beer "bits."
- Woodstock Bourbon and Coke RTDs – two 4 packs of 440ml cans, 5% alcohol, can be had for a total of NZ$22. That equates

to about NZ$1.60 per standard drink including 250ml of carbonated water and sugar "bits."
· Black Box Shiraz – 3 liter bag in a box, 13.5% alcohol, for a total of NZ$15.99. Simple arithmetic reveals that this is $0.55 per standard drink and only 100ml of water and grape "bits."

So what does all this mean?

Well, if you are a cost-conscious young drinker, and you don't want to spend half the night in line for the toilet, Grape-a-hol is your best bet by a margin of more than 2 to 1 on both price and surplus fluid disposal requirements. And, of course, there is the classier image of a wine glass as opposed to an overflowing and frothy beer mug or phallus-shaped glass bottle.

If you are a young woman who wants to enjoy a nice buzz and to reinforce feminine mystique, as well as reduce time spent in the much longer lines at the ladies room, is there really a choice? Further, if you have a preference for a sweeter beverage, a little doctoring with Sprite gives you a refreshing spritzer and you are good to go.

Grape-a-hol has become the modern day equivalent of cheap jug wine and, like its ancestors, the least expensive form of inebriation. The percentage of alcohol per volume guarantees a quick buzz, making it the fastest and cheapest "legal" high. Distinctive flavors, aromas, and mouth feel are largely irrelevant. Artistry has no place in this context. Stripped of cachet, distinction, and perceptible quality, Grape-a-hol has become little more than an inexpensive delivery system for introducing alcohol into the bloodstream.

This is hardly the image of responsible and appropriate consumption of a beverage that has evolved over millennia of artisan crafting. Yet this is precisely the market positioning that has emerged for the Grape-a-hol product category, which increasingly competes with cheap beer to offer the highest return on alcohol and the lowest requirement for liquid waste disposal, all wrapped in a "sophisticated" drinking package.

A perfect storm of oversupply, taxation policy, hypocrisy, and political expediency has brought back two-fisted drinking, fostered over-indulgence, and diminished the cachet, the quality, and the economic viability of wine.

And who benefits most from selling that 3 liter box of wine? You guessed right; in the above example, the New Zealand government takes a whopping 62% of the retail price. The wine excise tax is $2.60 per liter and added to that is 15% GST (Goods and Services Tax). Slightly less than NZ$10 of the NZ$15.99 goes into the tax coffers and NZ$6.10 is split up among the retailer, wholesaler, winery, and the grape grower, who are then taxed again on their profits – if there are any. So how can you possibly make any money this way? The answer is simple – volume, and there are legions of Grape-a-hol producers creating marketing campaigns based on cute labels, clever names, and fantasy lifestyles to drive up demand for this alcoholic beverage made from fermented grape juice.

Does it not seem a bit odd that the New Zealand government and large factory producers would give lip service to responsible consumption and moderation, when tax policy fosters, and profit strategies are predicated on, large-volume production of low-cost wine and getting consumers to "responsibly" drink it all?

This kind of production, taxation, and marketing hypocrisy is so remarkable that one has to wonder if anyone in charge is actually paying attention to the real problem, instead of just listening to their own spin. Without hesitation or the slightest concern for contradiction, wine taxation policies have conspired to reinforce alcohol abuse by sending an audaciously mixed message that is simultaneously overt and subliminal: "Partake moderately of inexpensive alcoholic beverages that you can buy in volume and for which we drive up demand to sell in volume, because that is the only way we can make money and raise tax dollars."

A partial solution to the problem in New Zealand is embarrassingly simple. Since price-sensitive younger drinkers are at the epicenter of the problem, increasing the price of the product would influence purchasing behavior. Since producers won't do this for fear of losing share to cheaper imports or others willing to make lower-cost, lower-quality product, the only player in the game with the power to influence price is the government.

At present, in New Zealand the excise tax is not levied at the retail point-of-sale – it is levied at the factory. All the government would need to do is change taxation policy so that the advertised retail price of wine (and beer, spirits, and tobacco as well) could not include the taxation component. Given social responsibility and temperance concerns, adding excise and GST at the cash register (as it is in many other countries like the U.S.) and preventing below-cost discounting would have a far greater chance of influencing consumer behavior and tempering the wine industry's race to the bottom, where profits lie solely in huge volumes with razor-thin margins.

Is this a sensible way to address a critical aspect of the problem? Yes. Will it happen? No.

The political will to change the policy is constrained by an electoral process that does not allow politicians to do what is right vs. what will get them elected. It is far easier for elected representatives to preach moderation and ravage the margins of producers than it is to face thousands of voters angry because the price of "piss" has increased.

And so, a perfect storm of oversupply, taxation policy, hypocrisy, and political expediency has brought back two-fisted drinking, fostered overindulgence, and diminished the cachet, the quality, and the economic viability of wine – a truly dubious distinction for many governments and Grape-a-hol producers alike.

All of this brings us to the final and perhaps most dreaded alternative: Minimum pricing of alcoholic beverages.

In a January 6, 2012, piece about the economics of curbing alcohol consumption, *Washington Post* reporter Sarah Kliff quoted the Centers for Disease Control's figures for how much binge drinking costs the United States.[1] According to their numbers, excessive alcohol consumption costs U.S.$223.5 billion each year, mostly from lost productivity and increased health care costs. She also reported that a team of Canadian researchers have explored what impact setting minimum alcohol prices could have on costs. They found that governments could drive down drinking by setting higher minimum prices for alcohol, an approach that could be more politically feasible than taxing liquor.

As Kliff reported, "researchers Tim Stockwell, M. Christopher Auld, Jinhui Zhao and Gina Martin combed through historical data on minimum alcohol prices in British Columbia, where the provincial government sets a price floor for various liquors, beer and wine." Since minimum prices fluctuated over several decades, it created a natural experiment for examining what happens when alcohol is more or less expensive. They found that for every 10% hike in minimum alcohol price, people drank 3.4% less alcohol. For certain drinks, like wine, the effect was even more dramatic: Increases in the minimum price of wine by 10% correlated with an 8.9% drop in consumption. Beer, however, appeared relatively resistant to price fluctuations, with a 10% bump lowering consumption a paltry 1.5%.

The conclusion from this research is intriguing. Setting minimum alcohol prices could reduce excessive alcohol consumption, and the negative public health outcomes that come along with it. Also, such a move would be politically more acceptable than change in taxation policy. As the authors of the study argued, "Minimum pricing promises the twin advantage of greater effectiveness for health purposes and greater public acceptability." They added that the "strong evidence that hazardous and problem drinkers seek out the most inexpensive alcohol so as to maximize ethanol intake per dollar spent."

In the same piece, Kliff noted that England and Wales recently passed legislation that prohibited selling below-cost alcohol, and Scotland is considering a similar bill. Naturally, the move has come under fire from the alcohol industry there. The Scottish Whisky Association has been a particularly vocal opponent, stating that, "Minimum pricing will fundamentally damage the Scotch Whisky industry at home and abroad with negative consequences for the wider economy." If you insert the words "the profits of" in front of "the Scotch Whisky industry," you will have a better understanding of the likely basis of their objection.

The economic incentives in the wine distribution system are too potent to expect any participant to voluntarily change their behavior in the interests of social responsibility. Creating policy statements, publishing press releases, and adding warning labels about responsible consumption of alcohol may assuage the conscience of corporate leaders, politicians, and public officials who want to believe that they have done something about problem drinking, but the simple fact is it doesn't change behavior.

The research shows that minimum pricing does change behavior. But until government and industry officials accept this reality and find ways to influence the economic formula, either with price controls and/or changes in the point of taxation, all their comments about the importance of responsible drinking are frankly disingenuous.

CHAPTER 12

Harry Potter Has Nothing
over Biodynamics

O n an otherwise uneventful flight from New York to San Francisco recently, the nine-year-old girl sitting next to Mark excitedly described how she and her friends were going to dress in costume for the premier of the final film in the Harry Potter series. She then proceeded to relate the entire Potter story from beginning to end and explain the lessons to be drawn from the books and films. Despite an exhausting week conducting wine tastings in New York, listening to this young girl's enthusiasm was entertaining – even more so when she confided the following:

> "You know, there really are witches and warlocks."
> "Really?"
> "And magic spells."
> "No kidding? How do you know?"
> "I found their website on the internet. There are spells and everything."
> "Have you tried any of these spells?"
> "Oh, no. That's only for Wiccans who achieve the fifth level. And the online training is very expensive. They have gatherings and everything."

You don't have to be a nine-year-old girl to believe in magic. It's more common than you might realize.

When a colleague recently forwarded a web link with the ominous and tantalizing address of www.biodynamicshoax.wordpress.com, we just had to click on it to read the latest take on a home-grown industry scandal. The link led us to a blog by Stuart Smith, a respected member of the Napa Valley wine-growing community, who has a Master's degree in Viticulture and Enology from the University of California at Davis. The blog exposes the pseudo-science, superstition, and magical thinking underlying biodynamic viticulture and is bluntly titled "Biodynamics is a Hoax."

It's actually not difficult to induce superstition – especially in someone who really wants to believe in a magic charm.

Biodynamics is a method of organic farming that utilizes such practices as observance of lunar phases and planetary cycles and the use of incantations and substances prepared according to strict rituals. The philosophy underlying the practices may involve anything from traditional organic farming to astrology, homeopathy, voodoo-style rituals, and "geo-acupuncture." Biodynamic wine growers use preparations made from cow manure, silica, medicinal plants, and animal organs. Examples of these include:

- Cow manure buried in cow horns in the soil over winter, then dug up, stirred in water and sprayed on the soil in the afternoon.

- Yarrow flowers are wrapped in a stag's bladder, hung in the summer sun, buried over winter, dug up the following spring and mixed with the compost.

- Chamomile flowers are wrapped in cow intestine, hung in the summer sun, buried over winter, dug up in spring and inserted in the compost (the used intestine is discarded).

- Oak bark is placed in the skull of a farm animal, buried in a watery environment over winter, dug up in spring and mixed with compost.

Biodynamic practices like geo-acupuncture adapt Chinese feng shui to the vineyard. They involve placing sets of matching stones on the ground with the aid of a pendulum to restore the "cosmo-telluric" balance of a vineyard. And yes, if you want to try this and if your credulity has not been stretched past breaking point, you can buy the stones online.

Rudolf Steiner, the creator of biodynamics, developed a philosophy called Anthroposophy, which is a mix of mysticism and science. In an article in the *SF Weekly,* a San Francisco newspaper, Joe Eskenazi noted that Steiner taught that,

Human beings are as old as the Earth, and our earliest civilized ancestors, the Lemurians, had "jellylike" bodies and could move objects with their minds. Their descendants lived on the lost continent of Atlantis, where their bodies continued to solidify. We are currently living in the fifth post-Atlantean epoch, which began in 1413 and will continue to the year 3573.[1]

In an audacious attempt to create a new wine style, Claude Giteau adopted a rather "unusual" technique.

According to the Fork & Bottle blog, as of September 2009 there were 529 "Natural and Biodynamic" wine producers worldwide.[2] Most claim to have attained important benefits from these ritualistic practices – though some admit to using it as a marketing ploy to lure consumers who believe biodynamics produces better wine. Regardless of the purity of the winemaker's motivations, the results are seldom, if at all, replicable, almost always confounded, and never scientifically validated. For all we know the benefits may simply be the result of the very meticulous practices and attention to detail that often accompany biodynamic farming. The rest may be a harmless superstition.

It's actually not difficult to induce superstition – especially in someone who really wants to believe in a magic charm. Cognitive researchers have been able to demonstrate repeatedly that when the human mind sees a favorable pattern or connection between events, it formulates a belief and seeks information that confirms the belief, often ignoring evidence that contradicts the belief. This is how superstitions are born. It's not unlike the ball player who forgets to wash his socks, hits a home run wearing dirty socks, and decides not to wash them for the rest of the season. Rituals and lucky charms simply offer believers a sense of control in uncertain circumstances.

It should come as no surprise then that in the debate about biodynamic winegrowing and the environment, the battle lines have been drawn. The scientists among us are attacking what they see as unsubstantiated claims and results that cannot be reproduced. The biodynamics believers are holding their ground. They maintain that their close-to-the-earth, natural farming produces a better grape, a better wine, and (unspoken) better marketing. Biodynamic non-believers resent the claim of better wine and the supposed premium it is intended to get. There are consumers who insist they can tell the difference and professionals who insist that they are merely seduced by the mythology behind the marketing claims. The longer the debate continues, the more adamant each side becomes about its convictions.

For the record, we don't believe there is anything inherently wrong with rituals, unless they cause harm or blind us to truth. Does the New Zealand All Blacks rugby team win because they perform a traditional Maori haka before the start of each international match? Or do they win because they are usually the most fiercely conditioned, talented, and formidable force on the playing field?

Few observers of this fearsome haka ritual would deny that performing it at the start of the game in the presence of the opposing team achieves an important psychological advantage and emotional lift for the All Blacks. However, despite a winning record exceeding 75%, even the most ardent supporter would be reluctant to argue that performing the haka causes victories. Unfortunately, when it comes to biodynamics and similar environmental practices, this is exactly the kind of proof offered by zealous proponents, who seem to confuse "correlation" with "causation." And, unless you're prepared for a fight, our advice on this point is to never – and we mean NEVER – point out this error in reasoning to a practitioner of biodynamics.

Superstition or not, two things are worth noting. First, a lot of reputable winemakers follow these practices, despite the added labor and cost required. So, they must be getting something out of it, whether it's the emotional satisfaction some people derive from belonging to a group or the economic benefit of a marketing ploy. Second, it's clear certain biodynamic farming practices are fundamental to organic farming, in that pesticides are avoided, sheep are employed to keep down weed growth, and manure is used for fertilizer.

In fact, a careful examination of organic, biodynamic, and sustainable practices reveals that there is a high degree of commonality between these programs. Each is built on sound principles of balance, minimal intervention, and concern for reducing the harmful effects of farming on the environment. Each requires extra effort and care on the part of the practitioners, as well as adherence to rigorous standards. And each includes a certification program that involves documentation of practices and independent audits by trained professionals. Were it not for some of the unusual rituals, a casual observer would have a difficult time distinguishing one approach from another.

We all have biases. Our personal exasperation with zealous biodynamics believers and organic purists has less to do with their commitment, goals, and core practices than with their superstition, phobia, and pseudo-scientific beliefs. When claims of benefits are exaggerated, confounded, or exempted from a standard of empirical proof, we believe consumers and environmentally-minded producers lose. There is no place for silliness in the very serious battle for the future of the planet and we fear that some of the ideological hooey that infiltrates the discussion diminishes the cause for all of us.

This issue aside, we believe the overwhelming majority of artisan winemakers share a common concern for the environment and a deep respect for the soil, site, and climate upon which they depend to grow their grapes. Ecological balance is more than a social responsibility to artisan winemakers, it is good grape-growing and winemaking practice. And since many live on or near their vineyards and wineries, it also is a very personal matter that has little to do with corporate marketing, public relations, or advertising hype.

CHAPTER 13

Claptrap about Closures

Quantum physics postulates the notion of the "multiverse," a hypothetical set of multiple parallel universes simultaneously similar and dissimilar to our own.

Question: In what universe do wine producers simultaneously ignore environmental harm, market perceptions, and quality?

Answer: This one.

Attitudes vary by country, but the preference for cork closures for more expensive fine wine or for certain events or occasions is undisputed.

Environmental Harm

In 2008 a comprehensive and independently peer-reviewed life cycle analysis on the environmental impact of natural corks, aluminum screw caps, and plastic closures was completed by PricewaterhouseCoopers and Ecobilan.[1]

The study found that CO_2 emissions – a key factor in climate change – resulting from the life cycle of a screw cap are 24 times higher than those from a natural cork stopper, while a plastic stopper is responsible for ten times more CO_2 than a natural cork. The study included analyses of seven key environmental indicators: The emission of greenhouse gases; consumption of non-renewable energy; consumption of water;

contribution to the acidification of the atmosphere; contribution to the deterioration of the ozone layer; contribution to eutrophication (nutrient build-up); and production of solid waste.

Cork stoppers emerged as the best alternative against six indicators and were placed second, behind aluminum closures, in relation to water consumption. Despite the clear evidence that screw caps are the most environmentally unfriendly wine bottle closure on the planet, there has been no appreciable shift away from screw caps by the wineries that use them, including those wineries touting their small carbon footprint. Further, there is little evidence fans of screw caps have toned down their rhetoric.

Setting aside the merits of different closures from the standpoints of wine protection and consumer perceptions of quality, why haven't more producers turned to closures that are responsible for fewer greenhouse gas emissions? Is it mainly, as we suspect, because screw caps cost less? Or are the advocates so emotionally and financially invested in screw caps that there is no path back? And finally, how does an environmentally conscientious wine consumer justify purchasing a bottle of wine under screw cap knowing that a screw cap is responsible for 24 times more CO_2 emissions than a natural cork?

Market Perceptions

The definition of "fine wine" may be up for debate, but when it comes to wines costing more than U.S.$25 per bottle the preference for closure type is not. In particular, U.S. consumers associate quality wine with cork – indeed a 2009 study suggested that 71 per cent of U.S. consumers *prefer* cork.[2] The researchers observed that "packaging can be of considerable value as a competitive marketing strategy" and that the "style of closure adds directly to the look of the product and is considered by consumers as a direct reflection of the quality of the wine." They also suggested that "consumers still consider screw caps to be an indication of cheap wines and cork an indication of quality."

Data reveal that attitudes vary by country, but the preference for cork closures for more expensive fine wine or for certain events or occasions is undisputed. For example, Australians and New Zealanders are more accepting of wine under screw cap, but they consider wine under cork more appropriate for a dinner party, special occasion, or gift. The bias of U.S. consumers was not lost on Nobilo, one of New Zealand's largest producers. In June 2009, *Decanter*, a leading wine magazine, reported the following:

Nobilo Marlborough Sauvignon Blanc became the first New Zealand wine to top varietal sales, taking over from perennial leaders Kendall Jackson of Sonoma County in an IRI sales survey for the month of April - figures were measured by volume."

According to Joe Stanton, chief executive of Constellation New Zealand, topping U.S. Sauvignon Blanc sales had been the company's main goal since launching the brand six years ago. "When we launched the brand we aspired to be the number one Sauvignon Blanc brand in the U.S., and to do that we had to focus on targeting what we saw as the 'traditional' U.S. wine consumers," he said.

To do this, Stanton said the company packaged the brand specifically for the U.S. consumer by sealing the brand under cork, a move that meant going against the dominant screw cap trend in New Zealand.[3]

"**Of course this is fine wine, sir. Would you care to sniff the screw cap?**"

Despite ample evidence of cork closure preference in the U.S. - especially as the price of the wine increases - in 2010 a group of 21 major New Zealand producers formed the "Complexity" initiative, "to establish New Zealand's credentials in the world of fine wine." They launched their first major event in Denver, Colorado.[4] "Born of intensive research," as one of the members stated, this group seems to have disregarded the market evidence that most U.S. wine consumers do not associate fine wine with screw caps.[5] Forty-nine of the 59 wines initially listed in the Complexity portfolio are sealed under screw cap.

In a moment of frank openness, the U.S. distributor for one of the 21 wineries privately admitted to us that selling that producer's wines under screw cap was an obstacle to sales and stated that it would be easier to sell if those wines were presented under cork. He also commented that "the less sophisticated the purchaser, the more they rely on the type of closure to signal the quality of the wine."

New Zealand's Complexity initiative with its mostly screw-capped wines reminds us of the Michael Crichton novel *The Terminal Man.* At one point two artificial intelligence computers are communicating. When one is offered a cucumber, which it is programmed to dislike, it responds by expressing dislike for cucumbers. The other computer, which is aware of the first computer's dislike and is programmed to be assertive, responds by saying, "I insist" multiple times, disregarding the first computer's preference. Then, the first computer, which originally had been programmed for politeness, says, "Go to hell."

However well-intentioned, the Complexity initiative appears to be disregarding an important preference in the U.S. by offering fine wine consumers more of what they do not want and taking the chance of effectively being told, "Go to hell," when the consumer buys something else. If this misalignment was confined to the 21 producers, it might be less of a concern. However, the Complexity initiative is heavily subsidized by the New Zealand government and it runs the risk of signaling to the U.S. marketplace that this is how all New Zealand wine producers think about customer preferences.

Wine Quality

As an artisan producer of fine wine, we have a practical disdain for cork.

After all the hard work we put into growing our grapes, meticulously sorting the harvested fruit, making the wine, barrel-aging it, bottling it, bottle-aging it, and then carefully selling it through costly routes to market, if we discover a bottle with TCA contamination, or cork taint as it is commonly known, we experience an irrational desire to drop napalm on the world's cork forests. However, to be fair to the cork industry, the TCA contamination rate is grossly overstated and is now probably less than 2% and even lower for higher grades of cork.[6] See the Cork Quality Council website (www.corkqc.com) for more information.

Despite our frustration with cork and our enthusiasm for the lower cost and convenience of screw caps, every single bottle of our carefully crafted Cabernet-blended wines goes out under the best cork we can find. Ultimately, we make our closure decision based on facts and reality – not wishful thinking. We consider three simple criteria:

1. Impact on quality of the wine during its intended life in the bottle.
2. Impact on the environment.
3. Impact on consumer perceptions and preferences.

What we don't consider is cost.

As noted earlier, the research shows screw caps are responsible for 24 times more CO_2 emissions than natural cork. Further, consumers in all markets do not associate fine wines with anything other than a high-quality cork closure.

When it comes to fine wine, particularly styles and varieties that spend years, if not decades, aging in bottle, high-quality cork is currently the superior closure. This is primarily because cork's minute gas permeability is believed to aid long-term micro-oxygenation of the wine which benefits maturation in bottle. Cork also does not contribute to reductive odors (rotten egg smell) that can result when wine is sealed with air tight screw caps. A 2009 study published in the *Journal of Agricultural and Food Chemistry*[7] reinforces cork's credentials regarding managed micro-oxygenation in wine. Also, a more recent study in the *American Journal of Enology and Viticulture* reported the impact of micro-oxygenation on the formation of reductive odors in Cabernet Sauvignon wines.[8]

So, until the screw cap's environmental credentials improve, until consumers no longer really care about the closure, and until the impact of screw caps on the aging of our style and type of wine is proven superior to natural cork, we will continue to stick a piece of highly refined tree bark in the neck of our bottles – and will suppress our eco-terrorist impulse if an occasional bottle of wine shows up tainted.

CHAPTER 14

Taint Is Not Flavor and Complexity Should Not Be an Excuse

While dining in a San Francisco restaurant recently, Mark overheard a curious exchange between a patron and a young server who had just poured a taste of a wine from a noted appellation. "What is that smell?" the patron asked. "Is this right? This can't be right. The wine list says 'rich, earthy, and complex.' More like moldy earth and compost. It smells like a stable. This can't be right."

The patron then took a cautious sip. "And it's sour. The description says 'chocolate, cherry, fig, and leather.' It should add 'sour and astringent.' Send the sommelier over. I want to watch him taste it."

Swallowing hard, the server responded with: "If the wine isn't to your satisfaction, I can bring you something else." The patron said: "Yes, I'll want something else. But, first I want to watch the sommelier taste this."

Most wine drinkers don't know that wine is composed of nearly a thousand compounds and not all of them smell or taste good, which probably is why drinking some wines occasionally requires suppressing a gag reflex.

If you ever find yourself wondering what experts mean when they refer to wine as "complex," consider this breakdown from Andrew Waterhouse at the University of California at Davis.[1] The major component of wine is water (about 85%), the second is ethyl alcohol (10-15%), followed by glycerols, and then tartaric, malic, latic, and succinc acids. Potassium, residual sugar (in some wines), phenolic compounds, and nitrogenous compounds round out the mix. Some of the "goodies" that have a disproportionate impact on color, flavor, and aroma are tannins, thioles, anthocyanins, esters, terpenes, and phenols.

Complexity does not, by definition, make the wine good.

These compounds come from both the raw material in the grapes and the process of making wine (vinification). The art and skill of grape growing and fine winemaking depends on how effective the winemaker and grape grower are at reducing, eliminating, or masking the "baddies" and accentuating the "goodies." It is not an easy set of tasks and decisions. The hard work begins each year when the vines are pruned during winter. It continues through selection of bunches during veraison, timing of harvest, fruit sorting during harvest, fermentation management, blending, and aging. What you see, taste, and smell is no accident – it is the result of deliberate choices made by both the grower and the winemaker. The microbiology of wine production is complex and the sensory experience of a wine is directly related to the quality of decisions made from grape to glass.

Some vineyards plant more for volume – high yield – than for quality fruit. They over-crop the vines, harvest mechanically, and sort fruit poorly or not at all. Inferior fruit, as well as compounds in the leaves, stems, insects, and rodents that find their way into the vats, impart elements that challenge even the most proficient winemaker to produce an untainted, fault-free wine. But that hardly matters when the wine is sold in bulk and is intended for consumers who are satisfied with an inexpensive alcoholic beverage that is an alternative to beer or ready-to-drink spirits.

The extent to which many of the compounds can make red wines taste good or bad depends on their concentration and "ripeness" (polymerization, for you chemists). Ripe tannins taste smooth and silky. Green or unripe tannins taste harsh and bitter. Some compounds can make the wine taste vegetal or herbaceous, even when present in trace amounts (parts per trillion). Interactions between compounds can add vinegary, sour, or moldy tastes, as well as discoloration and funky smells (think sweaty socks, mildew, sulfur, rotten apples, or barnyard).

There is one caveat here, however. Since wine preference is such a personal thing, "faults" can actually smell or taste appealing to some people. There is nothing wrong with diversity of opinion and preference among wine drinkers, but simply liking a faulty wine does not make it any less faulty. We think every wine enthusiast should draw the line when clear faults (volatile acidity, spoilage contamination, reductive odors, etc.) are touted as a distinctive "flavor" or offered as evidence of "complexity." The barnyard smell of high concentrations of *Brettanomyces* (one strain of wild yeast) in some wines is a notable example.

A sausage maker would blush.

For those unfamiliar with the standard wine faults, consider the following official list contained in the wine aroma identification kit "Le Nez Du Vin":

1) Vegetal	5) Soap	9) Cauliflower
2) Rotten Apple	6) Sulfur	10) Horse
3) Vinegar	7) Rotten Egg	11) Moldy-Earth
4) Glue	8) Onion	12) Cork

Regardless of the fact that some people find a few of these aromas pleasing, they still are considered standard wine faults and would prevent a product from passing export certification in some countries. That some wines make it all the way to bottle with one or more of these aromatic attributes is either a commentary on the frequency of sensory impairment in human beings or an indictment of manufacturing controls on the part of sloppy winemakers.

Contrast this with the list of 54 "pleasant" aromas in "Le Nez Du Vin":

1) Lemon	19) Apricot	37) Blackcurrant bud
2) Grapefruit	20) Peach	38) Cut hay
3) Orange	21) Almond (Kernel)	39) Thyme
4) Pineapple	22) Prune	40) Vanilla
5) Banana	23) Walnut	41) Cinnamon
6) Lychee	24) Hawthorn	42) Clove
7) Melon	25) Acacia	43) Pepper
8) Muscat	26) Linden	44) Saffron
9) Apple	27) Honey	45) Leather
10) Pear	28) Rose	46) Musk
11) Quince	29) Violet	47) Butter
12) Strawberry	30) Green pepper	48) Toast
13) Raspberry	31) Mushroom	49) Roasted almond
14) Redcurrant	32) Truffle	50) Roasted hazelnut
15) Blackcurrant	33) Yeast	51) Caramel
16) Bilberry	34) Cedar	52) Coffee
17) Blackberry	35) Pine	53) Dark chocolate
18) Cherry	36) Liquorice	54) Smoked

While these attributes are clearly more appealing, wines containing one or more of these aromas may still be faulty if testing reveals microbial contamination, an excessive level of volatile acidity, discoloration, or cloudiness. The interaction between positive and negative aromatic and taste characteristics can create some complex and strange combinations which challenge the limits of sensory description. However, that "complexity" does not, by definition, make the wine good. It often takes a trained and experienced palate to identify the underlying causes of complex faults that provoke one of the most feared and devastating sensory questions of all time:

"What IS that smell (or taste)?"

Making fault-free wine is a challenge in and of itself. Making a fault-free wine that can achieve a standard that earns critical praise for its balance, length, and complexity is an impressive achievement. That is why we find it particularly frustrating when wine critics, winemakers, and oenophiles miss obvious flaws, elevate taint to a "flavor," or use complexity as an excuse for poor quality control, microbial contamination, or manufacturing mistakes.

Whenever we hear someone argue that a particular fault adds "complexity," we cannot help but recall the comedian Jon Lovitz, who was a regular on *Saturday Night Live* in the 1980s. Lovitz often played a character named Tommy Flanagan, a pathological liar who would make exaggerated and patently untrue claims. When he'd finished constructing one of these outrageous stories and was satisfied with how it sounded, he would exclaim, "Yeah! That's the ticket!" as if it were now magically believable.

Wine appreciation is a very personal matter. It engages all of our senses. Different people like different things and diversity provides space for true creative expression in winemaking. However, when standard flaws are accepted as arguments for quality diversity, it diminishes the integrity of winemaking and the credibility of wine commentary for everyone.

CHAPTER 15

Wine Words:
Wacky, Witty, Weird, and Wild

In the never-ending search for new words to describe the appearance, aroma, and flavor of wine, we have been blessed with everything from delightfully imaginative comparisons to lofty terminology, arcane references, curious similes, baffling analogies, bizarre connections, and just plain wacky mind-benders. Wine writers, critics, judges, pretentious oenophiles, and more than a few winemakers all rack their brains, searching for the perfect descriptor in an apparent attempt to achieve adjectival nirvana.

If the public knew how Marvin composed his wine reviews, they would be horrified.

We cannot think of any product other than wine that has been variously described as biscuity, chewy, dirty, earthy, flabby, grassy, hot, inky, jammy, leathery, meaty, oaky, peppery, ponderous, smoky, unctuous, voluptuous, austere, corpulent, creosote, zippy, or laser-like. It often seems as if Dr. Seuss, the late American writer of fantastically rhymed children's books, has been resurrected to generate a vast cache of adjectives to baffle wine drinkers.

And when simple adjectives fail to achieve literary orgasm, less common or more arcane terms test the reader's knowledge, such as *réglisse*, maderized, and torrefaction. And, if that doesn't do the trick, new permutations are created, juxtapositions of words that test the limits of comprehension – "crushed stone," "peacock's tail," and "furry tannins."

The more adventurous and imaginative will even explore complex analogies and metaphors that push the boundaries of human experience, such as "cat's pee on a mulberry bush," "scorched earth," or "roundly ripened edges." The more extreme descriptors have encouraged humorous mimicry, including an online "Silly Tasting Notes Generator" programmed by Greg Sumner which is always good for a laugh.[1]

Others have taken this more seriously, such as Orin Hargraves, who in 2005 wrote the following about "whine writing":

> The other thing we observed about Pinot Noir reviews is that they are littered with notes: have you noticed? "Ripe cherry and red berry aromas and flavors pick up appealing bacon and mushroom notes on the finish." (With wine like this, who needs food?) "Spicy notes of oak, coconut, truffle, earth, smoke and briar dominate cherry fruit aroma." But what sort of notes are these? If they were on Post-Its you wouldn't be able to see the bottle. Note is a notorious polyseme in English, but we suspect that the writers mean the one you see off to the right there, "a characteristic emotional quality," though in the wine metaphor, emotion slips out and taste slips in. But we wonder: aren't these wines rather busy? Does a wine need so many notes? Add a few more and you'll need an index before you know it. If someone spoke "with notes of sarcasm, anxiety, gaiety, and delight over a subtext of pure vitriol" you would hardly be able to imagine it. We suggest that the quality, rather than the quantity of descriptive words about wine subtleties might serve the reader better.[2]

While we're on the subject of notes, it's worth noting that even popular music has been used to describe wines. Tom Wark shared the following description of a wine on his blog Fermentation and challenged his readers to guess the writer.

> The fruit here is not cherries or berries. This is rustic, earthy Pinot Noir. A good Savigny can bring to mind the song "Sweet Virginia," from Exile on Main Street, the one with the line about Got to scrape the something-or-other right off yer shoes. This Savigny takes us way down home. You can almost hear the pigs oinking and Howlin' Wolf's little red rooster crowing. Superb depth, long and full, delicious from start to finish.[3]

While the musical references and the description as a whole are fun to read, novel, and certainly memorable, we suspect it would leave many readers baffled. We have to admit, however, that it did pique our curiosity and we probably would buy the wine to match the experience to the description! By the way, the writer was Kermit Lynch, Wine Merchant, and the fascinating description appeared in his April 2006 Newsletter.

A New Zealand Sauvignon Blanc represented by a photo of crumpled newspapers, we assume, is more desirable than a Napa Sauvignon Blanc represented by a train wreck.

We're still not finished with novel descriptors, though. The Château Pétrogasm wine blog has come up with an even more challenging mode of evaluating and describing wine: Evocative photos and drawings. The Château Pétrogasm "residents" maintain that they provide:

> a valuable tool for wine drinkers by using colors, sketches, photography, and other visual media in order to convey both the intrinsic components of a particular wine along with a general impression of it. Wine is art; drinking it should be too! The serious problem with all wine reviews/scores is that they are inherently a personal opinion. Anyone can learn to taste wine. But, a review or score is based mainly on sensory perception and prior experience, both of which can differ dramatically between individuals and in combination produce infinite variability.[4]

They further argue that tasters mentally form visual images that offer an additional dimension from which to interpret and understand the experience of a particular wine. Therefore, communicating an evaluation with an image is a reasonable - if ambiguous - expression of the taster's experience. For example, a certain Bordeaux wine on the site is represented by a floating rose, defying gravity, while another is represented by a ripe, perfect strawberry, another by an architecturally elegant bridge, and still another by pencil shavings. Then of course there is a New Zealand Sauvignon Blanc represented by a photo of crumpled newspapers, which we assume is more desirable than a Napa Sauvignon Blanc represented by a train wreck, or the California Cabernet that is represented by a photo of a squatting toilet.

Some meanings are more obvious than others. Everything is open to personal interpretation. That is precisely the point. Whatever you think of this, the pure entertainment value is inescapable.

We often wonder if the best evaluations might be some combination of unique descriptors - whether words, music, or art with sufficient narrative to reduce ambiguity - which nevertheless leaves space for flights of fancy. We also agree with Hargraves that the quality of descriptive words is more important than the quantity.

Our personal preference is longer reviews that delve into the story behind the wine – the people, processes, and aspirations that influence the wine. How the soil, site, and climate contribute important and distinctive characteristics – in a word, "terroir." We are firm believers that wine lovers relish the story, nearly as much as they do the wine. Though there is rarely a moving story for Grape-a-hol, there is generally a deeper story to tell for artisan wineries. The question is whether it's crafted to suit the sensibilities and expectations of each audience and whether it brings to life an authentic and engaging narrative.

Naturally, the effort to construct such narratives and the time to read them is not compatible with supermarket-aisle economics or label-reading time constraints. Better to save the verbiage for those who have the time and interest in experiencing the whole package than waste it on those who just want to know if it is as good as the cute animal on the label and better than the bargain price on the sticker suggests.

CHAPTER 16

The Mantra for the Artisan Winegrower: Authenticity, Integrity, and Responsibility

We have covered a lot of territory in the previous 15 chapters, including why big corporations can't make fine wine, the truth about closures, the problems with wine competitions, the challenges of wine writing, and the conundrum posed by bulk wine. We have touched on wine taint, wine wars, and wine economy, along with the importance of terroir, the impact of environmental responsibility, how wine brands are burned in the supermarkets, and the false economy of cheap wine. We have butchered a few sacred cows, offended dilettantes, and assaulted some of the myths and institutions that have conspired to sacrifice the whole truth about wine at the altar of economic return.

Artisan winegrowers, it must be said, are a crazy breed of people, a mix of the truly inspired and the hopelessly delusional. They come from all walks of life, all professions, and all nationalities. They seldom have a clear idea of the true cost to make their product – mainly, we suspect, out of fear of knowing the answer.

Do artisans make better wine than the homogenized, financially driven, mass-market producers of Grape-a-hol? Many times, they do. Is the difference noticeable to the purchasing public? Even the neophyte drinker can discern the difference between a fine artisan wine and Grape-a-hol when they are put side by side. Otherwise, it depends on their expectations, motivations, and the frequency with which they drink fine wine vs. Grape-a-hol.

The artisan wine value proposition benefits everyone more than a price-slashing, margin-shrinking, tire-screeching drag race to the bottom of the price pyramid.

Sadly, as discussed earlier, one of the consequences of the proliferation of low-cost, low-quality wine is that some consumers have either acquired a taste for this beverage or developed a form of "cellar palate" that interferes with their ability to distinguish plonk from fine wine. Is it any wonder then why so many artisans who work hard to produce exquisite and expressive wines often feel like a piece of fine-grained leather at a Naugahyde convention? Consumers who have learned to value the price, smell, and feel of plastic are unlikely to appreciate the tactile and olfactory properties of genuine leather at any price.

Few people honestly expect Grape-a-hol to offer a sensory experience. For many consumers, it's simply an inexpensive alcoholic beverage for washing down dinner and relaxing with a light buzz. It's what they expect and what they get. If that is their motivation, they are getting what they paid for. Quality is not an important part of their satisfaction equation. For other consumers, Grape-a-hol is an inexpensive and effective way to imbibe a lot of alcohol and get smashed – solo or socially. Again, if that is their motivation, they are getting what they expected and paid for. Distinctive quality in these cases is less important than price and alcohol content.

Grape-a-hauling

Make no mistake, the overall quality of Grape-a-hol is at an all-time high compared to the "jug wine" choices of the past. Artisan winemakers frequently drink and occasionally enjoy it precisely for the purposes mentioned above. From the standpoint of value for money, there is no more economical or sophisticated standard drink on the market than Grape-a-hol.

But, does it qualify as fine wine?

Technical factors like balance may apply, but ultimately, the answer to that question varies subjectively with individual drinkers, their palates, their preferences, and their sensitivities. The difference between good and great or real and fake can be subtle. It can take a little patience and a discriminating eye – or palate – to detect the difference. The rewards for those willing to invest the effort are profound and sometimes life-changing from a sensory standpoint, a lesson learned at a very early age by Michael.

> When I was 12 my father announced that we would be living in England for a year. He was an artist and professor of art at the local state university. The purpose was to pursue research and hone skills.
>
> Our destination was a small town in southern England. We lived in a stately old mansion that was available in the off-season. My father set-up his studio in the formal dining room and my sister, brother, and I were enrolled in the local schools.
>
> At the end of the school year, we spent six weeks traveling through France, Germany, and the Netherlands. We visited some of the most famous museums in the world.
>
> One afternoon we were walking through the Rijksmuseum in Amsterdam. My sister, brother, and I were tired and starting to grumble after plodding through room after room of dark paintings, low light, and the smell of mold and centuries-old canvases. My father was oblivious, absorbed in masterpieces he had talked about for decades but never witnessed in person.
>
> I walked along trying to demonstrate some level of interest. The truth was I didn't really like any of the dark and somber old paintings of people dressed in strange clothing. Furthermore, I didn't really understand why they were masterpieces. They all looked very similar and the names were hard to pronounce – Rembrandt, Vermeer, Hals, Ruysdael, and others.
>
> In the center of one large room was a massive dark painting. It was more than ten feet high and probably 15 or more feet wide. A crowd was standing in front of it and speaking in hushed tones. It was clear that the painting was special. It had a prominent position, more people looking at it, and gold-braided barrier ropes kept observers at a safe distance.
>
> Despite all the cues that said this one is special, I did not understand why it was singled out. It wasn't any bigger, more colorful, or more interesting to me than dozens I had seen earlier.

My father was standing in the center of the room looking at this painting. I whispered, "What is so special about this painting?"

He bent over and said, "This is Rembrandt's The Night Watch."

"Why is it special?" I asked.

Without hesitating, he quietly said, "Look very carefully at the painting on the left and then look back at this one."

I stared at the painting on the left. After a few minutes searching for clues in this painting, I looked back at The Night Watch.

I was startled. I looked back at the painting on the left and then again at The Night Watch. It was astonishing. Even to a 12 year old.

To this day I cannot describe with justice the impact that comparison made on me. Although the painting on the left was itself a masterpiece, when compared directly with one of the really great Dutch master-pieces, it paled.

What made it different? It was not purely skill in painting, nor size, nor sub-ject matter, nor colors. It was a quality far greater and yet more subtle. Vibrance, emotion, a moment in time 300 years earlier captured for pos-terity. Something about that scene and that painting burned itself into my consciousness and left me with a powerful emotional memory that has survived for nearly a half century.

For the first time in my life I had experienced the true difference between something that was good and something that was great. I dis-covered that what separates the good from the great and the fine from the ordinary could be both subtle and profound, if you are open to it. That impression has never faded.

Artisan wines live at the creative intersection of subtlety, nuance, and passion. They strive for the great rather than the good, for artistry rather than ordinary. They provide a unique impression of the time, place, pas-sion, and aspiration of the people who grew the grapes and made the wine. To place artisan wines in the same category as Grape-a-hol would be like placing The Night Watch in the same category as wall paper.

But the challenge to the artisans is not to revolt or become what Michael Veseth in his book Wine Wars calls "terriorists," angrily decry-ing the sins of factory wine and clinging to antiquated rules or restric-tions to protect markets.[1] Rather, we think the moral high ground for the artisan winemaker is where it always has been – the soil, site, cli-mate, and aspirations of the people who see as their mission giving voice to the land through a very special beverage. To quote St. Ger-maine, "Wine symbolizes the alchemical marriage betwixt Heaven and Earth." Artisan winemakers are inspired by this notion and dedicate themselves to honoring the special connection between soil, site, cli-mate, and people.

It is true that economics play a significant part in artisan winemaking as well, but more often than not financial success is aimed at creating funds to continue practicing the craft. Perhaps one of the most common jokes in the industry is the story about the winemaker who won $5 million in a lottery. When asked what he was going to do with the money, he responded, "I am going to keep on growing grapes until the money runs out."

Unfortunately, unless artisans reclaim the high ground and connect with those who share the passion in what they do, the money will run out.

Around the world, small groups of artisan producers recognize the threat from the large mega-corporations producing Grape-a-hol, millions of liters at a time. They are banding together to try to protect and promote that which they feel is worth preserving. One such example can be found on a tiny island off the northern coast of New Zealand.

Waiheke Island is located a short ferry ride from Auckland, New Zealand's largest city. Situated in the Hauraki Gulf, Waiheke Island has about 7,000 permanent residents and is approximately 35 square miles (92 square kilometers). Martha's Vineyard in the U.S. is about two and half times larger in land area.

Waiheke has long been a holiday spot for New Zealanders and overseas visitors. The island's beautiful beaches, unspoiled bush, pastoral settings, picturesque bays, quaint villages, and hospitality services have made it a must-visit spot on every traveler's itinerary. It also is home to nearly 30 boutique vineyards and wineries, 24 of which are commercial businesses and members of the Waiheke Winegrowers Association. Many have cafés and restaurants which have achieved local and international acclaim.

As a winegrowing region Waiheke Island is tiny. With only 180 hectares of land under cultivation, it represents about 0.5% of New Zealand's plantings. And considering that New Zealand represents less than 1% of the world's production, Waiheke wine is indeed scarce. But what Waiheke producers lack in volume they make up for in diversity, quality, and yes, price. They are able to successfully grow 18 different varieties (12 red and six white). Seventy percent of the island's production is red varieties – principally dominated by Syrah and the five classic Bordeaux varietals (Cabernet Sauvignon, Merlot, Cabernet Franc, Malbec, and Petit Verdot). The white varieties are led by Chardonnay, Sauvignon Blanc, Pinot Gris, and Viognier.

Winegrowing on Waiheke Island is an expensive proposition. Land costs are high, labor is limited, and all supplies need to be shipped in from the mainland. As a result, Waiheke producers can't afford to make even average wine, which is why the local industry association took a bold step a number of years ago to protect the reputation, quality, and branding of Waiheke wine. As artisans, they recognized that the only economic platform they could stand on was quality and distinctiveness. Mother Nature did her part by providing them with the soil, site, and climate they needed to ripen red varieties, along with the tempering influence of a marine exposure. There is also the critical factor of small temperature fluctuations between day and night during veraison, which provides perfect maturation conditions for elegant and expressive fruit. It was up to the winegrowers to protect themselves against those inside or outside the association who would attempt to derive brand benefits without meeting minimum standards.

For this reason they developed the Certified Waiheke Wine[2] program. In fact, they were so committed to this standard that they changed their constitution and made compliance a condition of membership.

The principles of the Waiheke Certified Wine program are astonishingly simple and easy to understand by writers, consumers, and trades people alike. If you are going to produce a wine with "Waiheke" on the label, it must be made from 100% Waiheke Island-grown grapes, be part of a certified sustainable grape-growing program, and have been independently verified as free from standard wine faults as defined by the New Zealand Food Safety Authority as a condition of export. In this age of spin, hyperbole, and misrepresentation, the Waiheke Certified Wine mark is simple, clear, and compelling: A fault-free, sustainably grown, 100% Waiheke wine.

Imagine if every group of artisan winegrowers around the world were able to make and enforce a similar claim about their wines and region. Since much of the mass-produced wine involves deceptive labeling, massive amounts of blending from different regions, and questionable quality, a program like this would help consumers know when they were getting the real thing from real artisans. And for those to whom this matters, this message resonates.

This point of view is reinforced by a recent poll of U.S. consumers conducted by Public Opinion Strategies.[3] They found that Americans in particular feel strongly about the importance of location in making wine-purchasing decisions. Key findings from the poll of 1,000 U.S. wine drinkers were:

- 79% consider the region where a wine comes from an important factor when buying a bottle of wine;

- 75% report they would be less likely to buy a wine if they learned that it claimed to be from a place like Champagne, Napa Valley, or Oregon, but in actuality was not;

- 84% think that the region a wine comes from is extremely important in determining its quality;

- 96% say that consumers deserve to know that the location where wine grapes are grown is accurately stated on wine labels; and

- 98% support establishing worldwide standards for all winemakers that would require that they accurately state the location where wine grapes are grown on wine labels.

The poll was released by the signatories to the Joint Declaration to Protect Wine Place & Origin, a coalition consisting of 15 of the world's premier wine regions.

Rob Autry, a partner in Public Opinion Strategies and the lead pollster, stated, "In over 20 years of polling, rarely have we seen such strong feelings on an issue like this." He added: "Consumer sentiment this strong is a clear signal that Americans care a great deal about the location a wine comes from and clearly want ready access to that information when looking at a bottle."

Linda Reiff, executive director of Napa Valley Vintners, also commented on the results of the poll: "The research shows consumers are more focused on product origins than ever before and it isn't just a passing concern, but one they feel extraordinarily strong about . . . When a place name is misused, a part of the identity of that distinctive wine region is lost and consumers can be misled. This poll shows that U.S. consumers understand this and are looking for clear labeling of wine place names when they purchase wines."

The purpose of the coalition behind the Joint Declaration to Protect Wine Place & Origin is to articulate the shared belief that great wine is made in unique places all over the world and that these unique place names must be protected. "A failure to do so undermines all of these wine-growing regions and, as the research shows, runs counter to the expectations of the consumer," said Bruno Paillard, representing the Comité Interprofessionnel du Vin de Champagne. The coalition is committed to the assertive pursuit of truth in labeling and wine place names.

Authenticity is about truth - knowing that what you are purchasing is the real thing, not a clever substitute. Integrity is about sticking to your principles - even when it is inconvenient. And responsibility is about demonstrating concern for colleagues, customers, and the environment by what you do - even if it means delays and higher costs.

Authenticity, integrity, and responsibility are the pillars of true artisan winegrowing and the last line of defense against the rising tide of Grape-a-hol.

Our aim from the start of this book has been to influence the narrative about artisan wine and to make it clear to all that the differences between Grape-a-hol and fine wine are not just price and availability.

The fate of artisan winemaking rests with a larger group than the thousands of small businesses who practice this ancient craft. A large network of businesses and influential commentators wields considerable power over the industry. Their practices of late run the very real risk of starving the proverbial plow horse (see Chapter 7) simply to achieve short-term financial gains.

These influential interests include:

- The corporate producers who consider wine to be nothing more than a vehicle for profit making. Those who can rally the most capital, achieve the lowest cost of production, and capture the greatest control over the distribution system win.

- The taxing authorities who are motivated to increase government revenue while simultaneously preaching economic growth and drinking in moderation.

- The critics, wine writers, and promoters who devote time to rating mass-market wines better scored by a system similar to that used for grading meat.

- The large chain retailers who treat wine as a loss leading inducement for filling grocery carts.

- The distributors, arbitrageurs, brokers, and agents who, without remorse, willingly cannibalize a region, variety, or brand simply to make quick cash.

Ironically, what few of these industry players seem to realize is that the artisan wine value proposition benefits each of them more than a price-slashing, margin-shrinking, tire-screeching drag race to the bottom of the price pyramid.

If the trend continues, in the not-too-distant future the only people who will be able to produce or acquire fine artisan wines will be the very wealthy. The rest of us will retain an illusion of choice as we bob around on an ocean of sameness and battle the modern-day equivalent of the Hydra, the multi-headed beast of Greek mythology. When you lopped off one head of the Hydra, two more took its place. Our contemporary monster's head is composed of hundreds of colorfully labeled bottles containing 7.5 standard drinks of ethyl alcohol mixed with water and the equivalent of wine flavoring. Remove one of those bottles and two more quickly take its place.

However dismal this prediction sounds, the future need not be this bleak. Good people built the industry and good people can change it. In a recent blog post titled "What is 'Fine' Wine? Who Gets to Decide?", wine journalist Jamie Goode observes that:

> a new generation of wine people have emerged who seem to get wine – a group that encompasses winemakers, retailers, critics and agents. They have a more-or-less shared taste, in that they prefer elegance over power, dislike over-ripeness, delight in wines that express a sense of place, aren't afraid to explore new flavors and lesser known regions, and at the same time respect the classic European fine wines.[4]

These are encouraging words for artisan winemakers and their supporters. Real transformation in the wine industry is possible if the new generation of wine people presses for changes in tax and regulatory policy and insist that industry leaders protect national and regional provenance.

Elected officials need to replace outdated and parochial tax and regulatory policies that fail to address excessive consumption of wine. Changing the point at which taxes are levied or using minimum pricing and other anti-dumping regulations can have a profound affect on consumer behavior and discourage business practices that exacerbate the problem.

Likewise, wine industry associations need to diligently protect the value of their regional and national brands. Many of these national organizations have statutory power to levy their members. Along with that power goes an obligation to protect the brand assets over which the association has custodial responsibility. Too often these associations are excessively influenced by multi-national businesses with corporate agendas that are not aligned with national interests.

Artisan winemakers are not looking for special treatment, subsidies, or protectionist trade barriers. However, when tax, regulatory, and industry association policies conspire to exclude them from markets, burden them with punitive costs, and undermine the provenance on which their individual brands stand, they have a legitimate grievance.

By illuminating many of the wine industry practices that are often hidden from public view, we hope we have contributed to a better understanding of the challenges facing artisan winemakers and the options available for preserving a diverse and vibrant wine industry.

About the Authors

Michael F. Spratt, Ph.D., is a founder and owner of Destiny Bay Vineyards. Michael currently serves as President of the Waiheke Winegrowers Association, is a Director of New Zealand Winegrowers, and a founding member of The Specialist Winegrowers of New Zealand. Prior to launching Destiny Bay in 2000, he was a partner in mergers & acquisitions consulting for PricewaterhouseCoopers in their San Francisco office. In addition to his 20 year career as an international management consultant, he spent nearly a decade in production and business management in the micro-electronics industry in Silicon Valley. Michael holds a Ph.D. in Psychology from the University of California at Berkeley. He has written a number of articles on wine industry issues in New Zealand.

Mark L. Feldman, Ph.D., is the CEO of Destiny Bay Wine Imports. Mark has been instrumental in the marketing and branding of Destiny Bay Vineyards since its founding in 2000. His experience as the U.S. importer and distributor of New Zealand's highest rated artisan wine has made his presentation on luxury branding a featured attraction at private tasting events. He also is a former CEO of Space-Time Insight, a founding partner of Start Up Farms International, a Senior Vice President of Strategy at Virsa Systems and a Senior Vice President at SAP Labs. Earlier in his career he was a partner and global practice leader for mergers & acquisitions consulting at PricewaterhouseCoopers. Mark holds a Ph.D. in Communications from Northwestern University and is a frequently quoted speaker who has addressed audiences throughout the world on industry-transforming events.

Grape-a-hol is the second book written by Spratt and Feldman. Their first, *Five Frogs on a Log: A CEO's Guide to Accelerating the Transition in Mergers, Acquisitions, and Gut-Wrenching Change*, remains a business favorite in five languages.

About Destiny Bay Vineyards

Destiny Bay is a small, family-owned vineyard and winery on Waiheke Island, New Zealand, that specializes in estate grown and bottled blends of Cabernet Sauvignon, Merlot, Cabernet Franc, Malbec, and Petit Verdot. Destiny Bay produces fewer than 2,500 cases per year of their three distinct blends, Magna Praemia, Mystae, and Destinae. Acclaimed by international critics and collectors, Destiny Bay produces wine that prompted well-known Master of Wine and Master Sommelier Gerard Basset to rate them on par with French First Growths and Italian Super Tuscans. Destiny Bay is Waiheke Island's first fully certified Sustainable Winery & Vineyard (SWNZ) and is a founding member of The Specialist Winegrowers of New Zealand. Destiny Bay wines are available in New Zealand, Hong Kong, Australia, China, the U.K., and the U.S. For more information about Destiny Bay, the people, and the wine, visit www.destinybaywine.com.

Notes

Preface

[1] "U.S. Wine Industry Info." Retrieved from http://www.wholeworldwines.com/challenge/us-wine-industry-info/

[2] "Number of California Wineries." Retrieved from http://www.wineinstitute.org/resources/statistics/article124

[3] Lettie Teague, "Data Shows Growth in American Wineries" [blog post], January 24, 2012. Retrieved from http://blogs.wsj.com/wine/2012/01/24/data-shows-growth-in-american-wineries/

[4] Alder Yarrow, "The Future of Luxury Wine" [blog post], February 6, 2010. Retrieved from http://www.vinography.com/archives/2010/02/the_future_of_luxury_wine.html (comments made by Barbara Insel, President and CEO of Stonebridge Research Group at the Vino 2010 conference in New York).

[5] Paul Vigna, "U.S. Wine Trends Include Pending Grape Shortage, Increasing Demands for Wine," *The Patriot-News*, January 29, 2012. Retrieved from

http://blog.pennlive.com/wine/2012/01/us_wine_trends_include_pending_grape_shortage_increasing_demands_for_wine.html

[6] "U.S. Wine Industry Info." Retrieved from http://www.wholeworldwines.com/challenge/us-wine-industry-info/

[7] Alder Yarrow, "The Future of Luxury Wine" [blog post], February 6, 2010. Retrieved from http://www.vinography.com/archives/2010/02/the_future_of_luxury_wine.html (comments made by Barbara Insel, President and CEO of Stonebridge Research Group at the Vino 2010 conference in New York).

[8] Gil Gardner, "How To Find The Artisan Winemakers" [blog post], December 15, 2011. Retrieved from http://blog.vinnobles.com/2011/how-to-find-the-artisan-winemakers/

Chapter 1: 140 Forty Million Bath Tubs

[1] "U.S. Wine Industry Info." Retrieved from http://www.wholeworldwines.com/challenge/us-wine-industry-info/

[2] Adam Lechmere, "*Quarterly Review of Wines* folds," *Decanter*, February 1, 2012. Retrieved from http://www.decanter.com/news/wine-news/529698/quarterly-review-of-wines-folds

Chapter 2: Truth-Telling from Corporate Wine Closets

[1] Graham Holter, "Fine wine is not big wine, says Mondavi," *Harpers Wine & Spirits Trade Review*, April 29, 2010. Retrieved from http://www.harpers.co.uk/news/8962-fine-wine-is-not-big-wine-says-mondavi.html

2 Michael J. Mauboussin, *Think Twice: Harnessing the Power of Counterintuition*, Boston, MA: Harvard Business Press, 2009.

Chapter 3: The Plonk That Launched a Thousand Ships

1 "Wine Industry Titans Dispute Merits of Tanker Shipments," *Lodi News Sentinel*, October 10, 1957. Retrieved from http://news.google.com/newspapers?nid=2245&dat=19571010&id= o9o_AAAAIBAJ&sjid=3aMMAAAAIBAJ&pg=2683,5209403

2 Bob Hosmon, "Gallo tries to shed vin ordinaire look," *Lakeland Ledger*, September 10, 1992. Retrieved from http://news.google.com/newspapers?nid=1346&dat=19920910&id= 9ZFNAAAAIBAJ&sjid=OfwDAAAAIBAJ&pg=6919,5255056

3 For the plastic bladder, see "Liquid Container for Wine Transport." Retrieved from http://www.alibaba.com/product-gs/411354102/liquid_container_for_wine_transport/ showimage.html?newId=411354102&pn=1&pt=10&t=12&cids=. For the Containerpac, see "The video demonstration." Retrieved from http://www.containerpac.com.au/video/

4 Andy Hartley, *Bulk Shipping of Wine and its Implications for Product Quality*, WRAP, May, 2008. Retrieved from http://www.wrap.org.uk/downloads/Bulk_shipping_wine_quality_ May_08.7bb4eabe.5386.pdf

5 Kraft Foods, "Developing Markets' Growth Rockets Tang to 'Billion Dollar' Status," June 16, 2011. Retrieved from: http://www.kraftfoodscompany.com/SiteCollectionDocuments/pdf/ mmr%20Press%20Release%20Tang%20$1%20billion%20FINAL%20June%2014.pdf

6 United States Department of Agriculture (USDA), *Dairy: World Markets and Trade*, USDA, December 2011. Retrieved from http://www.fas.usda.gov/psdonline/circulars/dairy.pdf

Chapter 4: The Mouse That Tried to Roar

1 Wine Institute of New Zealand Incorporated, *New Zealand Winegrowers Export Monthly Report*, August 2006 through November 2011.

2 Penny Wardle, "Bulk wine conundrum here to stay," *Marlborough Express*, August 26, 2011. Retrieved from http://www.stuff.co.nz/marlborough-express/news/5512649/Bulk-wine-conundrum-here-to-stay

3 Penny Wardle, "Quality grapes earn no more," *Marlborough Express*, August 31, 2011. Retrieved from http://www.stuff.co.nz/marlborough-express/news/5539312/Quality-grapes-earn-no-more

4 "Brand PR failures: Perrier's benzene contamination" [blog post], December 5, 2006. Retrieved from http://brandfailures.blogspot.com/2006/12/brand-pr-failures-perriers-benzene.html

5 Dan Ariely, George Loewenstein, and Drazen Prelec, "Coherent Arbitrariness: Stable Demand Curves Without Stable Preferences," *Quarterly Journal of Economics* 118 (1), 2003, 73–105. Retrieved from http://web.mit.edu/ariely/www/MIT/Papers/CA.pdf

6 Russ Josephs, "The Grapes of Wrath: Chilean Wine Brands Taking a Beating," February 16, 2010. Retrieved from
http://www.brandchannel.com/home/post/2010/02/16/The-Grapes-Of-Wrath-Chilean-Wine-Brands-Taking-A-Beating.aspx

7 Daniel S. Putler, "Incorporating Reference Price Effects into a Theory of Consumer Choice," *Marketing Science* 11 (3), 1992, 287–309. Retrieved from http://www.kysq.org/docs/183891 .pdf

Chapter 6: Brand Burning in the Supermarkets

1 For more information see "Appellation d'Origine Contrôlée." Retrieved from http://en.wikipedia.org/wiki/Appellation_d%27Origine_Contr%C3%B4l%C3%A9e

Chapter 7: The False Economy of Cheap Wine

1 Christy Gren, "Bring it on! scream wine-lovers. Bumper profit-threatening harvest in New Zealand," *Industry Leaders Magazine*, February 12, 2011. Retrieved from http://www.industryleadersmagazine.com/bring-it-on-scream-wine-lovers-bumper-profit-threatening-harvest-in-new-zealand/

Chapter 9: The Hubris of Wine Writing: The Good, the Bad, and the Ugly

1 "Who we are." Retrieved from http://www.winewriters.org.nz/

2 "Empirical Foundations of Wine Expertise," *Australian & New Zealand Grapegrower & Winemaker*, 509, 2006, 115-117. (https://www.winebiz.com.au/gwm/view/?action=view&id=364)

3 Robert T. Hodgson, "An Examination of Judge Reliability at major U.S. Wine Competition," *Journal of Wine Economics* 3 (2), 2008, 105-113. Retrieved from http://www.wine-economics.org/journal/content/Volume3/number2/Full%20Texts/01_wine%20economics_Robert%20T.%20Hodgson%20%28105-113%29.pdf

4 Roman L. Weil, "Parker v. Prial: The Death of the Vintage Chart [Lighten Your Wallet]," paper given at the 8th Oenometrics Meeting of the Vineyard Data Quantification Society, Napa Valley, May 22, 2001. Retrieved from http://www.liquidasset.com/WEILVDQS.PDF

5 Liz Thach, "How American Consumers Select Wine," *Wine Business Monthly*, June 15, 2008. Retrieved from http://www.winebusiness.com/wbm/?go=getArticle&dataId=56883

Chapter 10: Wine Competitions and the Gambler's Fallacy

1 Liz Thach, "How American Consumers Select Wine," *Wine Business Monthly*, June 15, 2008. Retrieved from http://www.winebusiness.com/wbm/?go=getArticle&dataId=56883

2 Robert T. Hodgson, "An Analysis of the Concordance among 13 U.S. Wine Competitions," *Journal of Wine Economics* 4 (1), 2009, 1-9. Retrieved from http://wine-economics.org/journal/content/Volume4/number1/Full%20Texts/1_wine%20economics_vol%204_1_Robert%20Hodgson.pdf

3 Lenn Thompson, "We Won't Participate as Judges in Wine Competitions: Here's Why" [blog post], August 24, 2010. Retrieved from http://www.lenndevours.com/2010/08/we-wont-participate-as-judges-in-wine-competitions-heres-why.html

Chapter 11: Temperance, Tax, and Over-indulgence

1 Sarah Kliff, "The economics of curbing alcohol consumption" [blog post]. Retrieved from http://www.washingtonpost.com/blogs/ezra-klein/post/the-economics-of-curbing-alcohol-consumption/2012/01/06/gIQAv55ifP_blog.html

Chapter 12: Harry Potter Has Nothing over Biodynamics

1 Joe Eskenazi, "Voodoo on the Vine: The origins of the increasingly popular Biodynamic wine are steeped in the occult and bad science," *SF Weekly*, November 19, 2008. Retrieved from http://www.sfweekly.com/content/printVersion/1243412/

2 Jack Everitt, "Master List of 529 Natural and Biodynamic Wine Producers" [blog post], September 21, 2009. Retrieved from http://forkandbottle.com/wine/biodynamic_producers.htm

Chapter 13: Claptrap about Closures

1 PricewaterhouseCoopers/Ecobilan, *Evaluation of the Environmental Impacts of Cork Stoppers versus Aluminium and Plastic Closures: Analysis of the Life Cycle of Cork, Aluminium and Plastic Wine Closures,* October 2008. http://www.amorim.com/xms/files/CorticeiraAmorim/Noticias/ACV_Relatorio_Final.pdf

2 N. Barber, C. Taylor, and T. Dodd, "Twisting tradition: Consumers' perceptions of alternative closures," *Journal of Food Products Marketing* 15 (1), 2009, 80–103. Retrieved from http://www.tandfonline.com/doi/abs/10.1080/10454440802470615#preview

3 Daniel Pilkington, "Marlborough Sauvignon Brand Tops U.S. Market," *Decanter,* June 3, 2009. Retrieved from http://www.decanter.com/news/wine-news/484741/marlborough-sauvignon-brand-tops-us-market

4 "About Complexity." Retrieved from http://www.complexity.co.nz/

5 Tragon Corp., "Study: 94% of U.S. Wine Consumers Prefer Natural Cork, Wine with Cork Preferred for Gifts, Dinner Parties, Special Occasions Half of Respondents Say Screw-caps Convey Low Quality Wine." Retrieved from http://www.prnewswire.com/news-releases/study-94-of-us-wine-consumers-prefer-natural-cork-134819233.html

6 "Cork Quality Council Audit Results: Current Results from Screening of Incoming Cork Shipments Show an 83% Reduction in TCA," June 2011. Retrieved from http://www.corkqc.com/newsandpress/cnews2.htm. See also Amorim's *Bark to Bottle,* Issue #27, July 2010. Retrieved from http://www.corkfacts.com/publications/2010jul27.htm

7 Paulo Lopes, Maria A. Silva, Alexandre Pons, Takatoshi Tominaga, Valerie Lavigne, Cedric Saucier, Philippe Darriet, Pierre-Louis Teissedre, and Denis Dubourdieu, "Impact of Oxygen Dissolved at Bottling and Transmitted through Closures on the Composition and Sensory Properties of a Sauvignon Blanc Wine during Bottle Storage," *J. Agric. Food Chem.* 57 (21), 2009, 10261–10270. Retrieved from http://www.salcheto.it/spaw2/uploads/files/Journal Agriculture.2009.10261.pdf

8 Dang-Dung Nguyen, Laura Nicolau, Stuart I. Dykes, and Paul A. Kilmartin, "Influence of Microoxygenation on Reductive Sulfur Off-Odors and Color Development in a Cabernet Sauvignon Wine," *American Journal of Enology and Viticulture* 61 (4), 2010, 457–464. Retrieved from http://ajevonline.org/content/61/4/457.short

Chapter 14: Taint Is Not Flavor and Complexity Should Not Be an Excuse

1 Andrew L. Waterhouse, "What is in Wine?" Retrieved from http://waterhouse.ucdavis.edu/winecomp/index.htm

Chapter 15: Wine Words: Wacky, Witty, Weird, and Wild

1 Greg Sumner, "Silly Tasting Notes Generator 1.1." Retrieved from http://www.gmon.com/tech/stng.shtml

2 Orin Hargraves, "Whine Writing" [blog post], July 1, 2005. Retrieved from https://www.visualthesaurus.com/cm/ll/32/

3 Tom Wark, "The Art of the Wine Review" [blog post], April 6, 2006. Retrieved from: http://fermentation.typepad.com/fermentation/2006/04/the_art_of_the_.html

4 "About the Château and its residents." Retrieved from http://chateaupetrogasm.com/

Chapter 16: The Mantra for the Artisan Winegrower: Authenticity, Integrity, and Responsibility

[1] Michael Veseth, *Wine Wars: The Curse of the Blue Nun, the Miracle of Two Buck Chuck, and the Revenge of the Terroirists*, Lanham, MD: Rowman & Littlefield Publishers, 2011.

[2] "Certified Quality Marks Links," *Waiheke Island of Wine: Official Website of Waiheke Winegowers Association.* Retrieved from http://www.waihekewine.co.nz/Waiheke_Winegrowers_Association/CertifiedQualityMarkLinks.aspx

[3] The Joint Declaration to Protect Wine Place & Origin, "New Poll Shows Broad Support for Wine Truth-In-Labeling," PR Newswire, October 19, 2011. Retrieved from http://www.prnewswire.com/news-releases/new-poll-shows-broad-support-for-wine-truth-in-labeling-132139768.html

[4] Jamie Goode, "What is 'fine' wine? Who gets to decide?" [blog post], December 5, 2011. Retrieved from http://www.wineanorak.com/wineblog/uncategorized/what-is-fine-wine-who-gets-to-decide